THE SIX PERFECTIONS

D1603883

THE SIX PERFECTIONS

An Oral Teaching by
Geshe Sonam Rinchen

Translated and edited by
Ruth Sonam

Snow Lion Publications
Ithaca, New York

Snow Lion Publications
P.O. Box 6483
Ithaca, New York 14851 USA
Tel: 607-273-8519

Printed in Canada on recycled paper.

ISBN 1-55939-089-1

Library of Congress Cataloging-in-Publication Data

Sonam Rinchen, 1933-
  The six perfections : an oral teaching / by Geshe Sonam
Rinchen ; translated and edited by Ruth Sonam.
      p.   cm.
  Includes bibliographical references
  ISBN 1-55939-089-1 (alk. paper)
  1. Paramitas (Buddhism). 2. Perfection--Religious aspects--
Buddhism. I. Sonam Ruth, 1943-   . II. Title.
BQ4336.S66 1998
294.3'444--dc21   98-9466
                                                          CIP

Contents

Homage

With homage to Mother Teresa (1910-1997) and to the unnamed women and men of noble heart who throughout the ages have performed the marvelous deeds of Bodhisattvas.

> The fruit of silence is prayer.
> The fruit of prayer is faith.
> The fruit of faith is love.
> The fruit of love is service.
> The fruit of service is peace.
>
> — Mother Teresa

Acknowledgement

I would like to thank my editor Susan Kyser for her assistance.

Introduction

To dream of reaching a destination is not enough—you must pack your bags and set out on the journey. Bodhisattvas who are intent on enlightenment for the sake of all living beings make this a reality by adopting a certain way of life. All the advice the Buddha gave on this way of life and on the multifarious activities in which Bodhisattvas engage can be subsumed in the six perfections of giving, ethical discipline, patience, enthusiastic effort, concentration and wisdom. They comprise every practice needed to fully ripen oneself and others.

There are four principal ways of ripening others, or helping them spiritually to mature. This is done through generosity in order to establish a positive relationship with them, through interesting discussion regarding what is of true benefit, through encouraging them to implement what they have understood and by acting accordingly oneself. Since these activities are included within the practices of the six perfections, they do not need to be explained separately.

In his *Ornament for the Mahayana Sutras*[1] Maitreya explains why there are specifically six perfections and shows how they comprise all the Buddha's teaching on the conduct of Bodhisattvas. The great Tibetan master Tsongkhapa cites this work by Maitreya in his *Great Exposition of the Stages of the Path*[2] which will serve as the basis for the following explanation of the six perfections.

Maitreya points out that to accomplish the extensive practices in which Bodhisattvas engage for the attainment of ultimate well-being, namely an enlightened being's body, possessions, environment and companions, they need temporary well-being. This depends on an uninterrupted series of good rebirths in which they enjoy excellent conditions for continued spiritual practice, such as plentiful resources, a strong body and mind and supportive fellow practitioners. Nagarjuna's *Precious Garland*[3] defines temporary well-being or high status as the body and mind of celestial and human beings and the happiness they enjoy. To gain this we need faith and ethical discipline.

According to the sutras it takes many such rebirths to create the two great stores of merit and insight necessary for attaining enlightenment. If sutra and tantra are practiced together, enlightenment can be attained in a single lifetime by developing the kind of exalted wisdom which simultaneously and swiftly creates insight and merit. The ability to do this depends entirely on the high calibre of the practitioner and is firmly based on the three principal paths of insight—the wish to be free from cyclic existence, the altruistic intention and a correct understanding of reality.

Practice of the six perfections insures that we will gain an excellent body and mind and even more favorable conditions for effective practice than those we enjoy at present. The Buddha taught that generosity leads to the enjoyment of ample resources. Since human happiness is intimately connected with material well-being, the practice of generosity is explained first in the context of the six perfections, the four ways of maturing others and the three major ways of creating positive energy.

However, generosity cannot protect us from a bad rebirth in which it is impossible to make good use of these resources. Ethical discipline, another major way of creating positive energy, insures a good rebirth, while the practice of patience leads to an attractive appearance and supportive friends and companions. Cultivating enthusiastic effort endows us with the ability to complete what we undertake. However, even if we enjoy these conducive circumstances, our actions will not be effective so long as our mind is scattered and distracted by disturbing emotions. Fostering concentration, the third way of creating positive energy, makes our mind invulnerable to distraction. Unless we also possess the wisdom to discriminate between what needs to be cultivated and what must be discarded, we will consume the stock of positive energy created by previous wholesome actions without understanding what must be done to create new positive energy. By cultivating wisdom now we also insure that we will never lack wisdom in the future.

As practitioners of the Great Vehicle our wish to possess such an excellent body and mind is first and foremost for the benefit of others, and the six perfections play an essential part in bringing about their good. Through material generosity we alleviate their poverty and build up a constructive relationship with them, but if at the same time we harm them physically or verbally, our generosity will be of very limited value. Restraint from such actions is ethical discipline, which cannot be maintained if we respond to harm with the wish to retaliate. Patience thus acts as a vital support for the practice of ethical discipline. By not retaliating we prevent conflict from escalating and help our opponents not to create further negative actions. Our lack of vindictiveness may even win them over and present an opportunity to help them.

Enthusiastic effort is needed to complete what we undertake for others, while a stable concentrated mind and clear understanding of what is and is not constructive are also essential. The attainment of heightened concentration enables one to please and assist others through miraculous feats. Having made them receptive in these ways, wisdom is used in providing them with excellent advice, dispelling their doubts and showing them clearly how they can free themselves from cyclic existence. By fulfilling the needs of others through practicing the six perfections everything we wish for ourselves will be accomplished.

Each perfection is more difficult to practice and more subtle than the preceding perfection from which it develops. If we are not attached to what we own and do not seek to acquire further possessions, we are in a good position to maintain ethical discipline. While practicing non-violence, if we can tolerate suffering and bear harm both from the animate and inanimate, we can undertake any task without feeling discouraged. The resultant energy enables us to make joyous effort in positive actions of all kinds. These causes give rise to the single-pointedness of a calmly abiding mind which can be used for gaining special insight into reality.

Accustoming ourselves to giving will make us less attached to things. Guarding against carelessness through ethical discipline stops coarser forms of waywardness. The ability to accept and bear suffering prevents us from abandoning living beings. Unflagging enthusiasm is the way to increase virtue. Mental and physical pliancy attained through concentration stop disturbing emotions from manifesting, while close analysis increases wisdom and ultimately eliminates disturbing emotions and their imprints completely.

In general, practice of the first three perfections is particularly directed towards others' benefit, while practice of the last two is important for personal development. In both cases enthusiastic effort is vital, for freedom from both worldly existence and from a state of solitary peace is gained through wisdom, which requires the development of heightened concentration. This is impossible without enthusiastic perseverance.

The Tibetan words which are translated as "perfection"[4] mean "gone beyond." These practices are called perfections because they are practiced by Bodhisattvas with the supreme intention of attaining enlightenment for the sake of all living beings. A perfection surpasses other practices in the way that exalted beings surpass ordinary beings, the ultimate surpasses the conventional, nirvana surpasses cyclic existence, and understanding surpasses nescience.

A Bodhisattva's practice of the perfections gives rise to complete enlightenment, a state beyond both worldly existence and personal peace in which generosity, ethical discipline, patience, enthusiastic effort, concentration and wisdom have been perfected. Thus the cause is called by the name of the result. Practice of the perfections takes one to the other shore beyond the ocean of cyclic existence to a state in which the two kinds of obstructions—those to liberation, formed by the disturbing attitudes and emotions, and those which prevent complete knowledge of all phenomena—have been completely eliminated.

Chapter One

Generosity

Generosity is the willingness to give, and its practice consists of willingly giving one's body, possessions or positive energy. Simply overcoming miserliness, which is an aspect of clinging attachment, is not enough. Hearer and Solitary Realizer Foe Destroyers,[5] who have gained liberation from cyclic existence, have eliminated the disturbing emotions but have not perfected generosity. Its perfection is not measured by, for instance, how much poverty one has alleviated but by how complete is one's willingness to give. Clearly, however, generosity expresses itself in action.

How is generosity developed and increased? The first step is to think about the disadvantages of attachment and clinging and about the great benefits of giving. The Buddha stressed the importance of overcoming clinging to our body and life:

> When living beings cling
> To their ever-decaying body and life,
> Transient and beyond their control,
> Like dreams and magical illusions,
> They perform extremely unwholesome acts.

Under the influence of confusion
Their demonic mount bolts with the unwise
Into the bad state of the hells.[6]

Seeing the body as a putrefying mass of unclean substances
and recognizing that our life is unstable and our progress
towards death as relentless as a mountain torrent rushing
downhill lessens our clinging to them. Both our body and
life are governed by other factors in the form of compulsive
actions and disturbing emotions and have no independent
existence whatsoever but are deceptive like dreams and magical creations. Out of our attachment to them we perform many
negative actions and our mount, death, bolts with us into
bad rebirths.

The self seems to have independent and true existence but
is not as it appears. The body appears to be clean and plea-
surable but isn't. Our life-force seems to be enduring but in
fact is highly unreliable. These things are deceptive and all
the while our clinging to them stops us from being generous.
We act with miserliness because of the tight grasp we have
on our bodies and property. By overcoming attachment we
rid ourselves of a major source of strife.

Attachment to dwellings, places and countries causes conflict. No matter how hard we cling and try to resist change,
we cannot hold on to them because it is in their nature to be
unstable. Our body, possessions and dwelling places are ungrateful, for despite our efforts to care for them they automatically disintegrate and must be relinquished in the end.
Ridding ourselves of clinging to them is the best way to decrease anxiety and tension and to prolong our life. A short
life is the result of killing, an action which frequently is the
result of conflict rooted in attachment.

It is better to let go now before death forces our hand. There
is still time to extract some essence from what we own by
using it for the good of others. Though we are not yet ready
to sacrifice body and life, we can develop greater willingness

to part with what is ours. Give what you can now and make a strong wish to become able to let go of what you find most difficult to relinquish.

Bodhisattvas practice generosity and the other perfections with six kinds of excellence: they maintain the excellent motivation to attain enlightenment for the sake of all living beings. They incorporate as many excellent features into their acts of generosity as they can and, though they give only what is appropriate in a particular situation, they cultivate the readiness to give everything—body, possessions and positive energy. They practice as many forms of giving as possible, such as giving not only things but instruction and protection, to perfect their generosity and make it complete.

Their excellent aim is to bring living beings temporary and ultimate happiness. They employ the excellent skillful means of a conceptual or non-conceptual understanding that nothing has inherent existence. They make an excellent dedication for the benefit of all living beings and practice excellent purification in that everything they do is intended to eliminate obstructions formed by the disturbing emotions which prevent liberation and the obstructions which prevent knowledge of all phenomena. Even if we are not already Bodhisattvas, we can begin to emulate them.

The practice of any perfection incorporates the other five. Generosity alone will not protect you from the bad rebirths which result from negative actions. For instance, although you give when requested, you may feel tempted to speak harshly if the recipient shows dissatisfaction with what you have given, demands more or tries to return your gift. You need patience when faced with such an ungrateful or provocative response, otherwise anger will destroy the virtue you have created.

Don't lazily put off a generous action but enthusiastically seize every opportunity that presents itself. Appreciating the benefits of giving and the drawbacks of miserliness, concentrate fully on the generous action you are performing. Your practice of generosity must be wise: it is essential to have a clear understanding of what is appropriate to give, to whom and under what circumstances. Also remember that the giver, the gift and the recipient are dependent on one another and lack intrinsic existence. Even giving a handful of food while remembering these principles becomes an excellent practice.

Lay-people may find it easier to give protection and material help while, in general, it is easier for the ordained to give spiritual instruction, but this does not preclude lay-people from giving such advice. It is a mistake for ordained people to give up teaching and instead try to acquire material goods or amenities for others, since many actions contrary to the code of discipline for the ordained may be created in the process. An ordained person's main tasks are to study, listen and think about the teachings, to meditate and practice concentration in order to overcome what needs to be eliminated and to work for the spiritual community. Ordained people should be engaged in at least one of these activities. On the other hand, if an ordained person has ample resources, it is a fault not to use these to help others. If you really want to give, you will give whatever you can. Owning a lot is useless if your hands are tied by miserliness.

In his *Compendium of Training* Shantideva[7] mentions four additional factors which apply to the practice of all the perfections. Giving is the first factor and refers to a willingness, for example, to give your body or physical energy. Protecting is the second factor and involves not sacrificing your body until the time to give it has really come. You should only give your body when you can do it as easily as you would give someone a vegetable. When vegetables are scarce, as they are sometimes during the monsoon season in India, you might feel reluctant to part even with them!

The third factor is to keep your generous action pure from the polluting presence of disturbing emotions. The final factor is to insure increase. This could be taken to mean that by using your present body and mind well and generously, you insure good future rebirths in which you will enjoy a long life, an attractive appearance, good status, wealth, power, credible speech and a strong body and mind.

The same four factors apply to giving possessions, which should not be squandered but safeguarded until you have the opportunity to give them to those with great qualities, those who have helped and been kind to you or those who are suffering and in need. Purity in this context signifies that what is given should not have been acquired by wrong means, such as by deceit or extortion. Increase occurs because the more you give, the more resources will come your way.

Give the virtue you have created by dedicating it to the happiness of others. Since anger destroys virtue, protect it by practicing patience and keep it pure by insuring that neither self-interest nor concern for the well-being of this life adulterate it. Increase the virtue by rejoicing in the good you have done.

Generosity is universally praised in all spiritual traditions. Approaching it in these ways enriches your practice and makes it more profound, while certain thoughts and attitudes undermine it. Adherence to aberrant ideologies may lead one to believe that practicing any of the three forms of generosity is fruitless or that inflicting harm, for instance through ritual blood-sacrifice, is an appropriate gift to the gods. One may give in the belief that it will bring good luck or free one from attachment or think it proper to give protection to a single being at the expense of many others.

Give without humiliating the recipient of your generosity, without condescension, competitiveness or pride in giving more lavishly than others or in bestowing more effective protection. The conceit of thinking, for instance, that one gives the best teachings, uses the most eloquent language to communicate them or has the deepest grasp of the meaning spoils one's generosity, as do thoughts of the greatness and fame one hopes to achieve. Showing disdain for the miserly when one is generous may anger them and lead to their bad rebirth.

Give with joy and without discouragement at the thought of giving even as liberally as a Bodhisattva. Avoid feelings of incompetence and regret after being generous. Sometimes people give lavishly in a moment of drunken generosity and regret it later when they are sober! Take delight in the act of giving and overcome reluctance and aversion when called upon to be generous.

Bias in wanting to give only to friends and loved ones but not to enemies must also be avoided. We don't like to give anything to those we dislike and even feel irritated when someone else is generous with them. Try to give to friends and family without attachment. To those who harm you give with love, and to those who have neither helped nor harmed you give not with indifference but with affection.

Giving silver in the hope of receiving gold, thinking of the future riches one's material generosity may bring, hoping to become a great scholar because one gives teaching or to be powerful because one gives protection turns one's generosity into a business venture. In his *Yogic Deeds of Bodhisattvas*[8] Aryadeva says:

> When one thinks that by giving gifts now
> There will be a great result,
> Receiving and giving are like trade
> For profit, which will be criticized.

Nevertheless the fact remains that any karmic seed which is planted will grow and proliferate if it remains undamaged, just as in nature a single seed can produce a healthy plant with many uses and bountiful fruit from which will come many more seeds.

There are three thoughts to cultivate: when we are asked for something, it is a wonderful opportunity to perfect generosity which leads to enlightenment. The teachings, things or protection which others request in fact already belong to them because as practitioners of the Great Vehicle we have promised them everything we own and they are merely claiming what is theirs. The person who makes the request is our teacher of generosity.

Generosity is of true value when it is wholehearted. To teach what is easy but conceal what is profound shows a lack of generosity. In teaching a craft, for example, it is important to pass on everything one knows and not to withhold essential instructions for fear of being surpassed by one's students. It is inadequate to give only partial protection when one has the ability to do more. Often people keep things until they go bad or until their expiration date has passed and only then give them to others. Such gifts fail to bring joy because nobody likes to be given bad or worthless things.

Our generosity is directed to all living beings, who may be grouped into ten kinds: enemies, friends and neutral people, those with and without special qualities, equals, inferiors and superiors, and those who are happy and unhappy. To people with special qualities, such as those maintaining ethical discipline, give with liking and respect and give with compassion to the suffering or the unethical. Give without pride to inferiors, without jealousy to superiors and to equals without trying to impress. Give with love to the harmful and with equanimity to the helpful, always maintaining a lack of bias. Then dedicate the merit and the fruit of such generosity for the good of the person who requested help and for the happiness of all living beings.

Never disparage, mock, denigrate by innuendo or intimidate the recipient of your gift. Give from the heart with a smile, with sweet and kind words and with respect. As a result you will receive friendly help and service in the future. By giving at the time when your gift is needed your wishes will be fulfilled. Many people acquire wealth and property but seem unable to retain them because they are stolen or destroyed. Not causing any harm when you give makes your future resources stable. Giving with your own hands insures that those resources will increase. Patiently bearing any difficulties which your generous actions entail causes you to be surrounded by affectionate people. How can you be sure that these results will follow? The connection between actions and their effects is complex and subtle, but thinking about these statements and observing your experiences will help you to develop greater conviction.

There once was a man who found it very hard to let go of his possessions. To overcome his reluctance he began by passing things from one hand to the other and eventually he became able to give with ease. If we have trouble being generous, we should begin by giving small things, of which we can easily let go. The daily offering of fresh water placed on Buddhist shrines is an easy gift to make, since most of us have no difficulty in parting with water, yet good clean water is a precious gift in a hot country.

If someone you know wishes to give but is hesitant to begin or doesn't quite know how, encourage them, for instance by saying, "I have some clothes to give away. If someone asks you for clothes, would you mind giving them these?" or "Please tell them to come to me." Sometimes only a little encouragement is needed.

When giving spiritual teaching or instruction, do so with the three features described before: remember that your aim is enlightenment, that what you give has already been dedicated to others and that the recipient is your teacher of generosity. With a pure intention communicate what you know as fully as possible. If, as a result, the other person becomes more knowledgeable or more capable than you, all the better. Bestowing vows of any kind also counts as generosity of giving the teachings. But you don't need to be an official teacher to give valuable advice to someone who needs help, seems confused or appears to be going astray.

Learning texts by heart or reciting them may also be regarded as giving the teachings, if it is done with the wish to benefit others. Reciting texts can benefit those who hear them. A pigeon used to spend the night perched on a beam in a monk's room. This monk began reciting the *Compendium of Teachings Sutra*[9] every morning before dawn. Up on the beam the bird heard this, but, depending on the season, when the monk had finished reciting half or two-thirds of the text it grew light and the bird flew away. Hearing the text purified many karmic obstructions so that the bird was reborn as a human who had faith in the Three Jewels and eventually became ordained. He is said to have been a disciple of the great Indian master Vasubandhu. Without having to make any effort to memorize it, he could recite by heart the part of the text he had heard repeatedly in his previous life.

Even if you live in a cave and have no students you could imagine giving teachings to the beings of the six realms through which you help them attain liberation. Too many people believe that they will find happiness through material possessions, but even when they get the things they desire they still feel empty and unsatisfied and their problems continue. The only way to rid ourselves of this deep dissatisfaction is through inner changes which come from practicing the teachings. Nowadays an increasing number of people sense this and long to receive spiritual instruction but lack the opportunity. I have encountered groups of people who are eager to practice meditation. They meet once or twice a week but nobody has any clear idea how to bring about genuine inner transformation. Imagine yourself confidently giving them instruction and guidance.

Giving protection includes helping those oppressed by despotic rulers, governments or criminals, those who have been attacked or are threatened by wild animals, wild animals themselves who belong to endangered species and all who are at peril from the elements, for instance those caught in floods or fires. We may not be able to do anything on a very grand scale personally, but we can be active in or contribute to organizations which have the expertise to help.

There are many opportunities in daily life to save small creatures from drowning, burning or being otherwise hurt. Millions of beings live in fear. Imagine rescuing them and making them safe and comfortable, freeing the thousands of fish caught in huge modern fishing nets, releasing battery hens or penned animals who never see the light of day. Imagine the fish gliding through the water and the animals in fields and pastures gamboling, playing and feasting on lush green grass.

It is certain that we must eventually leave our body, possessions, friends and relatives behind. We create many negative actions out of attachment and hostility because we see the roles of friend and foe as fixed. What we are attached to cannot accompany us when we go, but the negative actions we have created will. If we can rid ourselves of clinging now, we will be able to face the inevitable separation from what we cherish without difficulty or regret at death. The highest form of generosity is non-attachment. A snake sheds its skin without any attachment to it. How easy it would be if this is how we felt about our possessions.

If we understand impermanence and are genuinely compassionate, we will regard our possessions as others' belongings which they have entrusted to us for safekeeping and which must be returned to them. With that attitude our property will not be a source of anxiety. If instead of giving them away we hoard things at home, they must be protected and become a cause of worry, discontent and wasted time.

Once there was a greedy monk who found it hard to refuse anything he was offered. A friend decided to help him and said, "I'll give you lots of presents, but each time you must say 'I don't want it.'" At first it required a huge effort even to pretend he didn't want the gift, but with practice it became easier to say the words. In the end he was able to refuse with all sincerity and overcame his greed. We too can remind ourselves not to be greedy by saying, "I don't really need it." Miserliness, greed and possessiveness are aspects of attachment which distort the objects to which they cling. We can cherish people and things without these constricting emotions. True love and compassion are realistic, spacious and allow others freedom.

Material generosity consists of giving our body and possessions, food, drink, clothing, shelter, conveyances and so forth. Giving our body doesn't necessarily demand the sacrifice of our life and limbs. It can be the use of our physical strength to care for the sick or aged, temporarily to relieve others who do this or to help with different kinds of light and heavy work.

If we have possessions, it is hypocritical simply to imagine giving. On the other hand lack of possessions need not be an impediment to the practice of generosity, since we can imagine emanating many bodies and giving lavishly. In meditation we enjoy unlimited resources and can give all that is needed, for instance supplying whole refugee camps or countries where there is famine with cooked or uncooked food and fresh clean water.

What we give should cause no harm nor have been misappropriated by us but should have been acquired in ways that accord with the teachings. It should be in good condition and look, smell, taste and feel agreeable. As a result we will enjoy an attractive appearance, fame, joy and an enduringly youthful body in the future.

When asked for help, don't let others suffer first for a while or exploit them by making them do what is contrary to the teachings or to social conventions before you give. Do not promise a lot or something good and later give less or something inferior. Do not flaunt your generosity, make a big fuss about it or remind the recipient and others of how kind you are.

At one time while the great Indian master Atisha[10] was in Tibet he received offerings of barley from people living in Lhasa which he carefully stored in a temple. As his disciple Dromtönpa[11] was retiring to bed, he felt perturbed about Atisha's seemingly acquisitive behavior and decided that the next day he would find out from his master what he intended to do with this large quantity of barley. Early in the morning on his way to see Atisha he passed the temple and noticed to his amazement that all the barley was gone. When Dromtönpa asked Atisha what he had done with it, he merely said, "I'm good at giving."

Instead of giving everything at once, we may be tempted to give a little at a time over a long period to make the recipient indebted to us or we may feel stingy about giving what we receive and hoard it first for a while before giving it away. This taints our generosity.

Those in authority should not take advantage of their position to give the wives, children and property of others to those they favor or wish to impress. Nor should one coerce others to give or forcibly take what belongs to one's parents, family members or servants and use it as if it were one's own to give away. What one gives should not cause trouble nor have been obtained in ways that conflict with one's code of ethical discipline.

The ideal donor is someone who lacks greed and is endowed with the seven jewel-like qualities of the exalted ones: faith, ethical discipline, generosity, extensive learning, understanding and a healthy sense of shame and embarrassment. The finest motivation with which to give is the altruistic intention. When we practice generosity in meditation, we imagine ourselves as powerful Bodhisattvas with the altruistic intention to take responsibility for the beings of the six realms and with the capacity to bear that responsibility.

Give without fearing deprivation, without intending to fool the recipient, without dislike, anger, hesitation or distraction, without impatience if the recipient is ungrateful and without wishing to draw attention to his or her faults or deceitfulness.

Special effort is needed when you find things particularly hard to give or when you fear that you might go short yourself. You have been much richer and owned more splendid possessions in previous lives but have had to let go of everything and will definitely have to again, so why not begin now?

A shopkeeper has no trouble letting go of his goods when a customer makes a purchase because he receives money in return. Our aim is to dedicate body, possessions and virtue to others with the same ease but without any hope for reward. For instance, we might think that when our generosity comes to the attention of those in authority, they will think highly of us and reward us with goods and services. A generous action done with such expectations may bring the desired results but will not act as a cause for liberation or enlightenment, since it wasn't undertaken for that purpose.

Instead of harboring the hope for return, remember that those who seek your help lack happiness, are on fire with craving and are powerless to remove their own suffering. Seeing this, think of nothing but helping them. Without hoping that your action will bring you a good rebirth or wealth, think only of highest enlightenment.

There is no need to give if the request is made to test or exploit you, if it is made by someone insane, if you are asked for profound or secret teachings by someone who is not ready for them or if you sense that the other person simply intends to use the information for commercial purposes or personal fame. Nor should you agree to a request if you suspect that there is trickery involved. For instance someone may ask for a statue, claiming that they are doing practices connected with the deity it represents and that they wish to make prostrations and offerings to it, but you may suspect that they actually intend to sell it. Both in real life and in imagination generosity requires the exercise of wisdom and intelligence, without which we may do more harm than good. In his *Summary of the Stages of the Path*[12] Tsongkhapa says of generosity:

> Giving is a wish-granting jewel
> Fulfilling the hopes of living beings,
> The best weapon with which to cut the knot of miserliness,
> A Bodhisattva action which gives rise to indomitable
>   courage
> And spreads one's fame in the ten directions.
> Knowing this the wise follow the good path
> Of completely giving body, possessions and virtue.

Chapter Two
Ethical Discipline

The role of ethics is important whether one is a lay-person or ordained. As humans we are capable of distinguishing between appropriate and inappropriate actions. Those which bring both immediate and ultimate happiness are clearly beneficial and wholesome. Those that bring happiness neither now nor later are indisputably unwholesome, as are those which bring only short-lived pleasure but ultimate detriment. Simply following our desires and acting impulsively without such considerations lands us in trouble. Whatever harms us and others is non-virtuous, while whatever benefits us and others is virtuous. This is worth bearing in mind.

Although generosity will bring us future resources, these will be wasted unless we can use them in a human or celestial rebirth. Faulty ethics lead to a bad rebirth in which we can only use up the fruits of past virtue but cannot accumulate fresh stores. A dog may live in luxury as an outcome of past generosity; it may look nice and be liked and cosseted by everyone as the result of practicing patience in the past, but it is still only a dog, incapable of discriminating between wholesome and unwholesome actions.

In his *Letter to a Friend*[13] Nagarjuna tells the king:

> Keep your ethical discipline pure,
> Free from degeneration and decline,
> Unadulterated and unstained.
> As the earth is for the animate and inanimate,
> Discipline, [the Buddha] said,
> Is the basis of all good qualities.

Nagarjuna advises his friend not to let his ethical discipline degenerate by making mistakes nor decline under the influence of the disturbing emotions. Neither should it be adulterated by the presence of attachment. Thinking only of liberation, he should keep it pure without allowing it to be polluted by worldly concerns. The Buddha used the analogy of the earth, which supports everything animate and inanimate, to illustrate that good ethics are the essential ground for the growth of all noble qualities.

Having established your criteria, remain mindful of them and check your thoughts and actions repeatedly during the day. When you feel tempted to do something negative, your sense of self-respect as a decent person and so-called practitioner will be a helpful constraint. Also reflecting on how the action would appear to those you admire has a restraining effect. Conscientiousness in preventing faulty actions leads to ethical discipline, which is your true protection. If people lived by such an inner code of discipline, there wouldn't be any need for law-enforcement on such a vast scale.

We hope for and speak of peace and happiness, but as long as we don't begin to create peace within ourselves, our hopes are futile. Lack of attachment to one's own side, lack of antagonism towards the other side and lack of confusion regarding what should be cultivated and discarded are the foundation for peace. Tolerance and patience don't arise from the suppression of anger, which simply goes underground and persists as resentment. Since no true peace and harmony are possible while resentment smoulders, effort to achieve conciliation and understanding is of vital concern.

A Bodhisattva's ethical discipline takes three forms: restraint from harm, creation of virtue and work for others. The latter two depend upon the first. Our perfection of ethical discipline is not measured by how successful we are in stopping violence or unethical behavior in the world, but by how developed are our personal intention and ability to refrain from harm.

A Bodhisattva's ethical discipline of restraint from faulty action is the intention to stop doing anything which is of harm to others and to dispel the source of that harm. Harm here refers primarily to seven harmful physical and verbal activities: killing, stealing, sexual misconduct, lying, harsh speech, divisive speech and meaningless speech. Killing injures the body and life of others, while stealing robs them of their property. Sexual misconduct exploits others, sullies their purity and arouses disturbing emotions from which unwholesome actions arise. Lying deceives others. Divisive speech turns friends into foes and further estranges those already on unfriendly terms. Harsh and abusive language hurts and upsets others, while idle talk distracts them and wastes their time. These physical and verbal actions are forms of violence and spring from three harmful mental states: covetousness, harmful thoughts and wrong views.

Restraint from these activities is not a practice confined to beginners. Those of intermediate and great capacity also practice it with different intentions, such as the wish to gain personal freedom from cyclic existence or to attain highest enlightenment for the sake of all living beings. For those who hold any form of the individual liberation vow, restraint from harm is practiced by observing the vow. For those who do not, practice entails restraint from these unwholesome physical, verbal and mental activities.

A piece of jewelry may look good on one person and not on another, but ethical discipline is an adornment which suits everyone, whether young or old, lay or ordained. The fragrance of flowers is carried on the breeze only when it blows in a particular direction, but the sweet smell of ethical discipline spreads far and wide in the ten directions of its own accord. It makes one radiant and clears the complexion better than the best of lotions. If you don't believe that observing an ethical life-style affects our physical appearance, take a look at people who do a lot of killing.

In *Engaging in the Bodhisattva Deeds* Shantideva says:

> Understanding that special insight well endowed with
> Calm abiding destroys the disturbing emotions,
> First seek calm abiding, but for that accomplish
> Non-attachment to the world with intense delight.

Special insight into reality with a calmly abiding mind destroys the disturbing emotions. For the growth of such special insight we must first develop a calmly abiding mind. This heightened state of concentration can only be cultivated successfully if we are free from attachment to worldly concerns, the prerequisite for true ethical conduct.

The first step is to recognize and acknowledge faulty thoughts and actions as such, which very few people are willing to do. The Kadampa masters[14] watched all their thoughts and actions, putting aside a white or black stone as they occurred and making a tally at the end of each day. Many people keep a journal and carry it with them all the time. It could be used in a similar way by entering ticks and crosses. Then, at night, you can see how many of each there are. If there are more ticks, you can congratulate yourself, but if there are more crosses, you should gently remind yourself, "You're doing what you've always done. It's not surprising things are still the same. If you want them to be different, you'll have to change these habits."

Purify all faults daily before you go to sleep. The great Indian master Atisha set us an inspiring example in this. On the long journey to Tibet he would stop the caravan each time he felt he had committed a fault, and everyone traveling with him waited while he undertook purification practices before a stupa which he carried for this purpose. He was always conscious that death could come at any time and that unpurified negative actions would be a source of future suffering.

If you carefully watch your physical, verbal and mental activities, you will gradually learn to distinguish between wholesome and unwholesome ones. Cultivation of such mindfulness is also a useful foundation for meditative stabilization. In your meditation sessions recall your negative activities and purify them. There is no need to hold on to guilt and feel weighed down by it. You performed the actions and you also have the power to purify them, no matter how grave they are. Faults, mistakes and disturbing emotions are not an integral part of our nature but temporary blemishes which can be removed.

In the practice of ethical discipline one tries to avoid faulty actions, but when they do occur one takes steps to purify them. The strongest antidotes are the altruistic intention and the understanding of reality. Since these clear away all obstructions to enlightenment, they certainly have the power to purify negative actions.

The four important counteractions are the power of reliance, the power of counteractive behavior, the power of regret and the power of the promise. All negative actions are created either in relation to the Three Jewels or to other living beings. Those created in relation to the Three Jewels—the enlightened ones, their teaching and the spiritual community—are purified in reliance on them by taking heartfelt refuge. Those created in relation to other living beings are purified by wishing to help them and by arousing the altruistic intention.

Counteractive behavior is any positive action undertaken as a purificatory measure. This may consist of prostrations or offerings, cultivating compassion and love, or it can be any consciously kind-hearted action. Contemplating that the doer of the negative action, the action and the object in relation to which it was performed are all interdependent and empty of intrinsic existence is the most effective counteractive conduct of all, since it gets at the very root of our negative actions, the ignorance which is the source of all disturbing emotions.

The power of regret involves acknowledging that we have performed a wrong action and recognizing that it will bring suffering if left unpurified. Feeling as though we have accidentally swallowed poison, we intensely regret what we have done. If this regret is genuine, the power of the promise not to repeat the action follows naturally.

A negative action has four effects. For instance, in the case of killing, the suffering we cause as we kill a living creature results in a bad rebirth. This is the action's fruit or maturation. We have shortened the life of a living being, which results in an experience similar to the action performed. After the bad rebirth, when we are once more born as a human, our life will be shortened by sickness or by an accident. The worst effect is the tendency to repeat the negative action again, which builds up the instinct to kill. By killing we rob a living being of its splendor. This produces the environmental result that we are forced to live in an unpleasant place which lacks any natural beauty.

Each of the four antidotes purifies one of these effects. The power of reliance purifies the maturation, for by sincerely taking refuge and arousing the altruistic intention we close the door to bad rebirths. Counteractive behavior purifies the experience that resembles the causal action, since the creation of virtue gives rise to agreeable experiences. The power of regret purifies the instinct to repeat the action because it reinforces dislike for what was done, and the power of the promise purifies the environmental result through interrupting the continuity of non-virtue. Conscientious application of these four is essential because we often perform negative actions out of the sheer force of habit. We must know clearly what is negative, develop a strong wish not to do it and express that wish through prayer.

It is excellent if you have a spiritual teacher to whom you can turn for advice and to whom you can acknowledge the mistakes you make. If you don't, act as your own teacher. Acknowledge your faults and mistakes before an image of the enlightened one or before other holy objects, and scrupulously apply the four antidotes.

Anger is easy to recognize as negative because it never feels agreeable, but desire and attachment fool us because initially they seem so pleasant. We can effortlessly remain absorbed in the object of our passion for hours on end without feeling at all tired. On the contrary, we find it stimulating. The more we think about it, the stronger our desire and attachment grow, but ultimately these emotions destroy our peace and lead to all kinds of unwholesome actions. If we are genuinely interested in overcoming them, we must, despite our reluctance, think about the ugliness or the drawbacks of the object on which these emotions focus. At least we could try to distract ourselves by turning our attention to something entirely different.

Everyone who hasn't yet rid themselves of the disturbing emotions experiences them, but most people find one to be much stronger that the others. For some, clinging attachment, desire and other associated emotions are the predominant problem. For others it is hostility and anger or it may be envy, jealousy and competitiveness or pride and arrogance. You must identify your particular troublemaker and work on that emotion.

If you wish to help others you must become sensitive to their personalities and perceptive about their disturbing emotions. Below the surface most people are unhappy. You may try to help with the best intention, but if you appear too competent and successful at managing your own life, your presence may depress the other person even further. If you admit you don't know all the answers, communication becomes more honest and probably more productive.

The importance of respecting others, of not being hostile, angry or dissatisfied with them is often stressed. Would ethical discipline towards others come more naturally if we stopped feeling dislike, anger, dissatisfaction and lack of respect towards ourselves? Feelings of self-hatred, dissatisfaction, anger and lack of respect directed towards ourselves, despite appearances, actually stem from our attachment to the self and to our happiness.

We hunt for happiness, hoping to find it through someone or something else. We are ignorant of the best and wisest way to cherish ourselves, and our clinging to a distorted idea of the self and to the happiness we desire for that self fills us with expectations regarding what we want to be and have. When we fail to meet these expectations, we feel dissatisfaction and a profound sense of failure. To fulfill the expectations would require not only many conducive circumstances but also tremendous effort, which we find hard to make. This leads to frustration and anger, which we turn against ourselves. Cultivating a sense of satisfaction and having few desires is the secret to peace and happiness. This is not an excuse for laziness. Where the well-being of others is concerned, we should certainly not be content with little.

While feeling frustrated and discontented we cannot enjoy our own company. Apparent self-hatred stems from an exaggerated preoccupation with ourselves, which gives rise to defensiveness, hostility and a sense of alienation. If we begin to feel differently about ourselves, we will be a lot more relaxed and less inclined to violent attachment or aversion, which are based on unrealistic projections. These are deep-seated problems for which there are no simple remedies.

In his *Letter to a Friend* Nagarjuna tells the king:

> The Subduer said care is the source of nectar,
> Carelessness the source of death.
> Therefore to increase virtuous conduct
> Always take interest in cultivating care.

Care and conscientiousness are cultivated by employing mindfulness and mental alertness and by developing a sound sense of self-respect and decency to guard the mind from the tyranny of the disturbing emotions.

Conscientiousness in resisting the disturbing emotions is the source of the nectar of immortality because it enables us to gain freedom from cyclic existence. Otherwise we continue to experience many forms of pain and suffering associated with birth, sickness, ageing and death and the frustrating situations we encounter. Cultivating such conscientious care in preventing disturbing emotions leads to true ethical discipline, the root of all happiness. While ethical discipline mainly concerns our physical and verbal behavior, our state of mind influences all we do. Use this pleasant garden of your precious human rebirth to cultivate the three kinds of ethical discipline until they flower and fruit in the state beyond sorrow.

Having laid a foundation of restraint from harm, begin to build up positive energy by constantly strengthening your ethical conduct and by training in concentration and wisdom. When you have taken a large loan from the bank, you have to repay it before you can begin to save any money yourself. Once your investment account looks good, you can start to give material help to others. Similarly, restraint from harmful action is like basic repayment of the loan, the first step. Then you can begin creating a wealth of positive energy and use it to help others.

Though all three kinds of ethical discipline are practiced simultaneously, beginners lay greatest emphasis on the ethical discipline of restraint from harm, while new Bodhisattvas concentrate on the creation of virtue. Success in work for the well-being of others increases your interest in hearing, thinking and meditating. If the work you are doing proves useful, it is a mistake not to give it as much energy as you can, yet at the same time you should not jettison more contemplative activities but aim for a healthy balance.

When motivated by the altruistic intention, training in ethical discipline, concentration and wisdom as well as all positive actions or practices such as prostrations, circumambulations, saying prayers and reciting mantras are a Bodhisattva's ethical discipline of creating virtue. Much merit is created by venerating and serving those with special qualities, by appreciating and praising the marvelous qualities of the Three Jewels and by mentally and verbally rejoicing in the good done by others. Instead of retaliating when harmed, the situation can become a source of merit by regarding what has happened as the outcome of your own past actions. Sincerely dedicate all virtue you create and use it as a basis for heartfelt prayers of aspiration. Be conscientious in seeking ways to create fresh virtue and to sustain and enhance virtue already created, so that the flow is never interrupted. Also guard the doors of your senses.

Through the senses we experience sights, sounds, smells, tastes and tactile sensations as attractive, unattractive or neutral. We respond to what we find attractive with desire and craving, to the unattractive with aversion or hostility and to the neutral with indifference and confusion. Guarding the senses entails preventing such disturbing emotions in response to sense stimuli. The Kadampa master Geshe Bengungyel[15] said, "I stand at the doors of my house with my spear at the ready. When the disturbing emotions turn aggressive, I'm aggressive too, but if they relax, so do I."

Why are the disturbing emotions indicted as the archvillains? Because they make the mind unpeaceful, turbulent and unserviceable. When they are active we feel restless and upset and express this in words and actions that disturb others. Neither we nor they thrive on this. When our mind is free from disturbing emotions we feel serene and happy. Our physical and verbal behavior expresses this and brings joy to others.

The Buddhist teachings help us clearly to identify these disturbing emotions, how they arise and how they affect us. The teachings also provide us with methods to make them subside, to prevent them from occurring and to uproot them completely. If we take their advice to heart, it will help us deal with everyday difficulties. What is the use of spiritual practice that promises future happiness but does not help us now? The Buddhist teachings offer a medicine to cure our present ills and keep us healthy. Whether we take it or not is our choice.

The teachings are not a system of rules nor a fixed code of conduct to which we must adhere. They provide us with the means to alleviate our own and others' suffering. Football players follow rules. They understand them well and know how to implement them, but what they do is not a spiritual practice. Spiritual practice consists of knowing the teachings and implementing them in such a way that they bring about an inner transformation, extending our perspective beyond its present narrow limits.

Virtue can be accumulated through quite mundane activities like eating and sleeping. Eating moderately with the purpose of nourishing and strengthening the body for practice and offering the first part of our food and drink to the Three Jewels creates merit. Wrong eating habits weaken the body and are an obstacle to meditation. Although this is self-evident, many people have serious problems with regard to their intake of food or are tempted to eat what they know will not agree with them. We should also sleep moderately, ideally devoting the first and last parts of the night to practice and sleeping only in the middle.

Most of the methods for creating virtue can be integrated into daily life. For example, offerings can be made anywhere, both actually and in imagination. Analytical and placement meditation should both be cultivated daily. Analytical meditation, for which everyday events present constant opportunities, is especially important for beginners because it is particularly effective in bringing about transformation. It is used to arouse positive feelings and induce insights, which are then sustained through placement meditation. It takes continual effort to remain conscious of our physical, verbal and mental activities, but this is necessary because our habits are deeply ingrained. As we keep doing it, it becomes easier.

The Kadampa master Geshe Sharawa said that if we leave the spiritual teachings aside, we will have great difficulty finding any other better means to happiness in this life. Moreover, the teachings are the only way to insure future happiness. Disturbing emotions and compulsive actions must be vigorously counteracted because a gentle indulgent approach will not get rid of them. They won't take pity on us and leave us alone. We must be undeterred and persistent, otherwise every relapse will dishearten us. Change occurs through courage and hard work because antidotes to the disturbing emotions do not grow strong of their own accord.

Hoping for help is not enough, since Buddhas and Bodhisattvas, who love us more than we love ourselves, cannot help unless we help ourselves. If it just depended on them, they certainly would not leave us in this predicament. They can show us what to do, but only we can do it. As soon as we begin, they wholeheartedly support our efforts.

As Mahayana practitioners our aim in everything we do is to alleviate others' suffering and bring them happiness. Thus restraint from harm and the creation of virtue are for the sake of others. We needn't be anxious that we will remain mired in suffering if we exert ourselves for them, because our own well-being is a natural by-product of our concern for others. Any help we give while motivated by the altruistic intention and holding the Bodhisattva vow constitutes the ethical discipline of working for others.

There are eleven major ways of assisting others. The first of these is to offer them our support in activities like accumulating, protecting and increasing wealth through farming, business and so forth, using only ethical means. Also included is support for those who suffer by devising ways to help the blind, deaf and infirm.

The second of the eleven ways of working for others consists of giving friendship to those who are confused. You may, for instance, help someone involved in a negative course of action to understand what is worth cultivating and what should be discarded. The many forms of counselling and therapy that are currently practiced can present the opportunity to introduce a spiritual dimension. They become Bodhisattva activities if they are accompanied by a true wish to help.

The third is to give friendship through offering service to others by such actions as welcoming strangers and providing them with accommodation, food or with whatever assistance one can.

The fourth is to help and protect those who fear harm from other living beings, whether humans, animals or spirits, or who are in danger from the elements. The list of things people fear is endless. Some fear the dark, others are afraid of spiders, of being in a crowd, of loneliness or of being without a trusted friend. There is no denying that many terrifying things exist in the world, but at the root of all these fears is self-concern. How do we deal with fear? Specific fears have specific causes which must be addressed, but in general it is true that the more we let go of our self-concern, the more fear decreases.

The moment we hear of any disaster, we think, "What if this happened to me?" The self-concern at once draws the disaster into its orbit. It is useful to think about karma and how one never experiences the effects of an action one hasn't performed. Thinking that any fear we experience is the result of having caused others fear in the past can also be helpful. Much that we fear has little external reality but is created by our minds. We train ourselves to let go of fear and to become more courageous and relaxed by thinking, "I'll manage somehow." There are many situations in which we can protect ourselves from fear simply by being sensible, but when we cannot cope alone, we should not hesitate to seek the help of others. It is important to recognize our own limitations.

The fifth way of helping others is giving support and consolation to those grieving over the loss of or separation from parents, children, partners, trusted friends, spiritual teachers, possessions or wealth. This requires skill and empathy. Sometimes it may be possible to create some breathing space by reminding the bereaved person that loss and separation

are a natural part of life and inherent in everything impermanent. While it is important not to suppress grief, grieving
can be destructive when too intense and prolonged.

The sixth is to give support to those in material or spiritual need. This may be done by providing them with neces-
sities, such as food, clothing and shelter, or by giving them
guidance and advice.

The seventh is to support those who have different kinds
of aspirations. This might involve helping them by ethical
means to find employment, achieve status or acquire things.
However, not all aspirations deserve support! In the case of
someone who is overcome by lust, teaching them to meditate on ugliness may be necessary. When we are infatuated,
we see only what is attractive and exaggerate that. Gradually we discover faults as our infatuation grows weaker. Meditation on ugliness merely hastens this process, not by fabri-
cating ugliness where none exists, but by focusing on aspects
which the infatuated mind disregards.

The eighth is to give support in keeping with others' dis-
positions and capacities by helping them to overcome hindrances to their immediate and long-term well-being through
methods which are appropriate in each particular case.

The ninth is to support those who are engaged in constructive activities. This means praising and encouraging those
whose conduct is admirable, who are engaged in hearing,
thinking and meditating, who have developed insights and
wisdom or are kind-hearted and compassionate. We are often reluctant to do this and instead subtly denigrate their
achievements. We begrudge others their happiness. For instance, when someone we know receives a gift and joyfully
shows it to us, we manage to deflate their happiness by point-
ing out some defect. Why not add to their happiness by praising it?

The tenth consists of giving support by castigating those
who are engaged in detrimental activities. This may entail
taking stern measures to stop them, since one should not con-
done or indulge others' fondness for harmful actions.

The eleventh is to give support by using any miraculous powers we possess to help others. This may include teaching non-verbally by demonstrating impermanence or the importance of wanting to free oneself from cyclic existence. Someone with miraculous powers might use them to frighten a wrong-doer by manifesting a hell-realm. Do you think that teaching on the fundamental nature of reality can be given non-verbally?

These different ways of helping others are practiced through analytical meditation, placement meditation and action. A Bodhisattva's conduct is rooted in the altruistic intention. The cultivation of kindness automatically prevents the infliction of harm. Although the conduct described here is that of highly accomplished Bodhisattvas, there is much we can already do to help others in similar ways.

A sincere desire to cultivate what is constructive and avoid what is detrimental leads to successful restraint from the ten harmful actions. As a result of familiarity with such restraint one will easily be able to follow a Bodhisattva's way of life in the future. Lack of restraint results in many faulty actions and an inability to keep promises and abide by commitments. In his *Summary of the Stages of the Path* Je Tsongkhapa says:

> Ethical conduct is water that washes
> The stains of faulty action, and moonlight dispelling
> The hot torment of disturbing emotions.
> Glorious like Mount Meru among those of the nine states,[16]
> Its power subdues all beings without use of threats.
> Knowing this the wise safeguard, like their eyes,
> The discipline to which they are fully committed.

Chapter Three
Patience

The essence of the Buddha's teaching is to avoid doing harm and to give help, both of which are impossible without practicing patience. If you are tempted to retaliate as soon as others injure you, you still have the impulse to harm. While you feel like harming others you cannot help them.

What is true patience and how can we develop it? Patience is imperturbability in the face of harm and hardship. Responding to these difficulties with anger is extremely destructive because it creates unpleasant consequences and destroys positive energy. There is no austere practice to equal the practice of patience, which calms the turbulence of the disturbing emotions. It is cultivated in meditation and implemented in everyday life. There are three main kinds of patience: the patience of taking no account of those who inflict harm, the patience of willingly accepting adversity and the patience of gaining certainty with regard to the teachings. Their opposites are animosity, discouragement and reluctance to engage with the teachings.

As a first step towards developing patience, think about its benefits and the drawbacks of anger, which has both visible and invisible consequences. The unseen effects of anger are that it destroys virtue accumulated over aeons. Anger directed at a Bodhisattva is particularly destructive, and since there is no easy way of telling who is and isn't a Bodhisattva, it is prudent not to get angry with any living being.

Patience must be cultivated constantly. This is the only way to be prepared when provocative circumstances arise. Try to prevent anger altogether, but if does arise, take steps to insure that it is short-lived and does not turn into resentment. You may be fully aware of anger's many disadvantages, but if you don't make a conscious effort to develop patience, you will still turn into a ball of rage every time you are provoked. Not expressing anger is no indication of patience, which is not the suppression of anger but the ability to remain calm and not get upset.

Anger robs us of our peace of mind, leaving no room for joy and happiness. Even the softest bed will not induce sleep when anger smolders. It makes us behave vindictively even to those who have been kindest to us. Through our irritability we lose friends and alienate people to such an extent that they will avoid us, though we may try to be generous.

Chandrakirti's *Supplement to the Middle Way*[17] says:

> It makes us ugly, leads to the unholy,
> And robs us of discernment to know right from wrong.
> Impatience quickly casts us into bad rebirths.

When the fire of anger burns, we grow ugly, hot and bothered and red in the face. Soon frowns, wrinkles and beads of sweat appear. Anger upsets us and others. We become incapable of distinguishing between right and wrong, and as a result we often make serious mistakes because our mind is not clear.

On the other hand patience gives rise to joy, happiness and well-being now. Its practice closes the door to bad future rebirths, creates the cause for a strong body and mind and eventually leads to liberation. Through it we develop the meditative stabilization of love. Serenity and joy make us attractive and radiant in a way that outshines conventional beauty. Gods and humans will love us and surround us with their friendship. Happiness is not fortuitous but the result of virtue, and nothing protects virtue better than the practice of patience.

It isn't enough to know the list of advantages and disadvantages. Think about them daily, until you really want to become more patient. Remember how you feel and look when you are angry. What a relief it would be not to keep getting upset but to enjoy peace of mind! The essence of the Buddha's teaching, particularly of the Great Vehicle, is love and compassion. The faults of anger are emphasized so frequently because anger is utterly contrary to the spirit of the Great Vehicle and to the practice of non-violence.

Compassion is finding it unbearable to see others suffer or create causes for suffering. Those others are not only humans, and the suffering concerned covers all levels, even the most subtle. Though words, such as compassion, used in different spiritual traditions are often the same, we must think whether their meaning and implications are in fact identical. Non-violence towards living beings entails not violating but cherishing even the water, earth, air and forests which form their habitat. There is much that each of us can contribute towards this ideal. When we do something we know to be harmful, we may feel sincere regret or be quite ruthless about the harm we do. Our regret will help to prevent us from repeating the action. Genuine non-violence, love, compassion and the wish to help are noble human qualities which anyone can develop, no matter to which culture they belong and no matter whether they are young or old. They are not the exclusive prerogative of Buddhists.

Only by identifying and stopping its causes can anger be overcome. The seeds of anger and other disturbing emotions continue to lie dormant within us until we have rid ourselves of them completely. When we encounter a stimulus and respond with an inappropriate and distorting mental approach the disturbing emotions arise. Although we harbor seeds for the whole gamut of disturbing emotions, they do not all manifest with equal intensity. Some people are calm and peaceful but quite confused and find it hard to learn anything new. Other people are quick to learn but easily irritated. Whatever our propensities may be, we are not condemned to remain as we are. Change is possible if we are sufficiently determined. Keep trying and remember that even the smallest progress is better than nothing.

Is anger towards inanimate objects as serious as anger towards living beings? Anger is always negative but is more dangerous when directed towards living beings. We may smash our best cups but they don't suffer. Afterwards, when our rage has died down, we may regret our bad temper and set to work with the glue.

The patience that takes no account of those that harm us is directed towards three categories of beings: those who harm us because we harmed them in the past, those whom we haven't harmed but who harm us and those who harm us despite our kindness to them. The last category demands the greatest patience.

Just as we cannot hold the ordination vow unless an abbot bestows it on us or the instructions for a practice unless a spiritual teacher passes them on to us, we cannot develop this kind of patience without someone to harm us. In this sense the harmful person is our teacher of patience. When Atisha set out for Tibet, he took with him one of his students, a particularly bad-tempered scholar. His other companions were very surprised and urged Atisha to leave him behind, but Atisha insisted, saying that this was his teacher of patience. The story goes that he sent the scholar home once they reached Tibet, the implication being that teachers of patience were plentiful there!

According to the *Great Exposition of the Stages of the Path* there are three points to consider in stopping anger: the object, namely the one inflicting harm, our subjective state of mind and the basis. Should you be angry with the people who harm you? Your immediate response is probably that anger is totally justified because they have intentionally hurt you, deprived you of happiness and made you suffer physically or mentally. But did they harm you of their own free will or not? You will find they didn't have any choice: the seed of anger was in them, a provocative situation arose, their mental response to it was distorted and as a result anger overwhelmed them.

Since others are enslaved by anger and are its victims, reciprocating with anger is an inappropriate response. An exorcist dealing with someone possessed doesn't get angry when the possessed person behaves violently, but tries even harder to drive out the evil spirit. The person inflicting the harm is like someone possessed or demented.

"But," you protest, "those who harm me are perfectly sane." Conventionally, that is true, but actually they are suffering from a far more pernicious form of insanity—the kind produced by the disturbing emotions—which has afflicted them throughout all their past lives and which affects their physical, verbal and mental behavior now, making them perform many misguided actions. Compassion is the only appropriate response. The parents of a demented child don't get angry when it behaves crazily, but only want to help it regain a sound state of mind.

Normally people try at all costs to avoid danger and harm to themselves, but because of anger and other disturbing emotions they will even slash their wrists, jump off cliffs or drown themselves. When normal inhibitions associated with self-preservation mean nothing to them, is it surprising if they hurt us? Rather than feel angry with those who harm us, we should feel sorry that they are profoundly unhappy now, are making others miserable and are creating the causes for future unhappiness.

Is the harmfulness an integral part of their nature or not? If it is an inseparable part of their nature, anger is an unreasonable response because they cannot help themselves. You don't get angry with fire when it burns you because it is fire's nature to be hot and burning. If that harmfulness is not an integral part of their nature but a temporary aberration, then too, anger is an inappropriate response. You don't get angry with the sun when a cloud passes in front of it. The harmful intention and the harmful activity are passing manifestations which occur only when certain temporary irritants are present.

Should I be angry with what is actually harming me or with what underlies the harm? In the former case I should be angry with the stick that beats me or the words that hurt me because they actually cause the pain. If anger towards the indirect cause of my pain, the person who employs them, seems more logical, I should reconsider. Surely the other person is not in control but is manipulated by a disturbing emotion, so my anger should be directed towards that.

The other's anger arises because the seed of anger is present, but this seed is only activated when provocative circumstances occur. I am the provocative circumstance which has triggered the anger, thus, in an indirect way, I have actually harmed the person who is injuring me and am responsible for his or her subsequent bad rebirth.

The Kadampa masters advise us to meditate on the arrow and the target as a way of considering the root cause of the painful situation. If we don't set up a target, there is nothing for the arrow to hit. Suffering is not uncaused nor does it come from incompatible causes but results from a compatible cause, a negative action created in the past. This is the target we ourselves have set up. The arrow that finds the target is simply a maturation of that past action. Our everyday experience substantiates this. If we behaved badly to someone yesterday, it probably won't be long before we experience the repercussions.

So far we have examined the question mainly in relation to the object. Now we consider the subjective aspect. If we cannot bear a relatively minor form of suffering, such as the hurt someone inflicts, our wish to retaliate is totally inconsistent because we thereby create the causes for much more intense suffering. It is foolish to behave in such an illogical way.

In his *Supplement to the Middle Way* Chandrakirti says:

> If you accept what is said about the ending
> Of the effects of past non-virtuous actions,
> Why attract the seeds of suffering
> Through harm and anger towards others?

A negative action we performed in the past resulted in a bad rebirth. The harm we experience now is the remaining negative momentum of that action. Why do we resent the person who helps us to end the effects of previous wrong-doing? In fact they are doing us a favor. We willingly undergo unpleasant medical treatment, even an operation, to avoid more intense suffering. If we try to retaliate when harmed, we simply perpetuate the whole cycle.

When people get angry with you, they often try to draw you into their dynamic. Should you leave as fast as possible, listen calmly, tell them their anger has got the better of them or acquiesce to their demands, thinking that the suffering involved is the remaining result of a previous unwholesome action you performed? Practicing patience means not getting upset and remaining calm but does not demand that you allow yourself to be manipulated or exploited by others and their disturbing emotions.

Telling others home truths while they are in a rage is counterproductive. Even being nice to them may simply make them angrier. It is probably best to leave them alone. Any discussion should take place when they are in a calm and rational state of mind. The painful situation is a result of our past actions, but we shouldn't seek more suffering as a way of ending the impetus of those actions. We should take steps to avoid further suffering and purify the underlying causes which could give rise to it, namely the imprints of past actions which have not yet borne fruit. When suffering is unavoidable, we should try to accept it as a natural consequence of what we did.

We should not waste our physical and mental energy on seeking out suffering nor on trivial pursuits, but should do what will bring lasting happiness, now and in the future. Our body is as vulnerable as a festering boil, ready to erupt into intense suffering at the slightest circumstance. It is difficult to take care of, its condition cannot be much improved and it is extremely fragile. Nevertheless, since we seek lasting happiness, which can only be attained through spiritual practice, we need this body and must look after it well. An analogy from Chandrakirti's *Commentary on the Four Hundred on the Yogic Deeds of Bodhisattvas*[18] speaks of a rich merchant's son who was tied to a thief. It isn't clear whether they were tied by emotional or physical bonds. Since the merchant wanted to look after his son, he was obliged also to look after the thief. If we want to take care of our spiritual interests, we need to take care of the body.

By practicing patience instead of getting angry, we come closer to enlightenment and create positive energy. Why should we feel angry with those who provide us with this opportunity? Those who hurt us and cause us suffering ignore the connection which exists between actions and their effects. If we retaliate, we are no better than they, since we also ignore it.

Hearers and Solitary Realizers, who are concerned with personal liberation, make great effort to overcome anger. To say we want to practice the Buddha's teaching, particularly that of the Great Vehicle, and hope to become enlightened in order to care for all living beings who are our mothers and yet to give free rein to our anger, thereby injuring others, is a contradiction.

Intelligence is needed to gain any form of knowledge and it is particularly necessary for the great transformation we hope to make through meditation. Compassion, love and patience can only be developed through intelligent analytical meditation. These feelings are then sustained by placement meditation. Analytical meditation enables one to prevent anger in the first place and to diffuse it when it does arise. The problem is that we aren't really willing to take the advice of the great masters to heart!

We may succeed in remaining calm in the face of provocation, but if others' praise, rewards, respect or service attracts and excites us, our practice of patience will not be trustworthy because the eight worldly concerns will prevent us from practicing purely. We like it when we and those we care for are happy, receive praise and rewards and enjoy a good reputation. We feel displeased and irritated when we or they are unhappy, are criticized or defamed or do not receive gifts and rewards. Where our enemies are concerned, we feel displeasure when they enjoy good fortune and pleased when they do not.

However, happiness, praise, reputation and rewards tend to make us arrogant, distract us from virtue, decrease our aversion to cyclic existence and increase our envy of those who enjoy these things in equal or greater measure. The more they mean to us, the more upset we feel when someone prevents us from receiving them. Only our own positive energy is of any true use and this cannot be enhanced by praise, reward or reputation, which can neither insure our long life, good health or physical strength nor help us in the future. They may bring us some short-lived satisfaction and joy, but better and more trustworthy sources of joy exist. Why do we get upset when what we crave eludes us? We are like children who build sand-castles, which are useless as dwellings, and who cry when they collapse or are washed away by the tide.

Far from getting angry with those who prevent you from receiving what you crave, be grateful to them because they protect you from a bad rebirth and insure that you have fewer enemies and fewer people who envy you. You are better able to concentrate on virtue, are less distracted by senseless preoccupations and can therefore more easily free yourself from the bonds of attachment, which closes the door to suffering. If you are not attached to approbation, you won't get angry when disparaged because you are no longer motivated by the competitive urge to outdo others or the need for acclaim.

When praised always assess whether the praise is justified and whether you actually possess the qualities for which you are lauded. If you do, rejoice without pride or conceit. When you are criticized, honestly examine whether or not you possess the fault. If you do, you can take steps to rid yourself of it. If you don't, the criticism is misdirected and nothing to get angry about because eventually its inappropriateness will become apparent to others. A more relaxed and easy-going attitude to both praise and blame will save you from much unhappiness and anger.

But even if you begin to feel a greater sense of equanimity about these matters, can you bear to see a friend or workmate receive an award or praise which you do not receive when you have both done the same work, and how do you respond when your enemy is mistreated or maligned? Reflecting on your feelings in such situations puts your progress into perspective.

The teaching on how to practice patience challenges us to act in a way which totally contradicts conventional norms of behavior. In the world praise, reward, respect and service are considered highly desirable, but the teachings draw our attention to the dangers which lie in our response to them.

To stop anger it is also essential to recognize and prevent its causes. At the root lie our misconception of the self and our self-concern. The self and its happiness appear all-important. Everything we call our own and see as contributing to that happiness must be guarded and protected. Anything we suspect could prevent or interfere with what we or those we care for want is a threat. Anyone who does or might do what we or those near to us don't want makes us unhappy. Unhappiness feeds and nourishes anger. That anger hurts others and often, too, we turn it against ourselves in an urge for self-destruction, which arises when we feel unhappy and worthless.

How do we prevent unhappiness? By consciously fostering and cultivating its opposite, happiness. When a situation makes us unhappy or has the potential to do so, the most important way to stop unhappiness is to overcome the tendency to reject what is happening. There is no need to feel unhappy if we can alter the situation. In that case our energy is best directed towards bringing about change. Obsessively thinking about how unjustified and unwanted the situation is absorbs our energy and prevents us from finding a way to resolve it. If we can do nothing to change the circumstances, our lack of acceptance and anxiety are useless and only add to our misery. By staying calm we are better equipped to deal well with the experience. The patience of willingly accepting hardship consists of turning difficulties we encounter into an adornment. If we want to be happy, we must work at stopping unhappiness.

When people speak unpleasant, demeaning, critical or disparaging words, they cannot harm our mind, since the mind is formless and immune to injury by words. Nor can they hurt our body. Realizing that we are actually invulnerable to those words makes us strong and gives unhappiness no opportunity to arise. We may recognize this, but nevertheless feel angry because those who make fun of us, disparage or defame us behind our backs turn others against us and prevent us from receiving the praise, rewards or popularity we desire. We must anyway leave honor and glory behind when we die but must experience the fruits of our anger in the future. It is better to die soon without praise, awards or renown, than to live long and create many unwholesome actions in the quest for what we desire.

We automatically feel displeasure when our enemies prosper and pleasure when their fortunes decline. Why can we not bear to see them thrive? It is inconsistent with our claim to be practitioners of the Buddha's teaching and followers of the Great Vehicle and incompatible with our ostensible wish to attain enlightenment for the sake of all living beings.

Many of us daily recite words expressing the intention to convey all beings to enlightenment, the highest form of happiness, yet we begrudge them the trifling happiness they derive from praise, reward and a good reputation. Why not instead, without envy, take joy in seeing them flourish? Good and responsible parents feel happy to see their children able to stand on their own feet. Since we have assumed responsibility for living beings, why not feel pleased when they do well? We are hypocritical and insincere if we don't. What use is our displeasure anyway? It won't prevent them from being praised, from receiving gifts or from enjoying a good reputation.

And why do we feel glad when those we dislike are in difficulty? We would be content to see them experience illness, loss of wealth and property, separation from friends and loved ones and various other calamities, but none of this will happen just because we wish it. Our malevolent thoughts harm us much more than they harm others. Even if these disasters befell them, what good would it do us? We might experience some fleeting satisfaction, but what is the use of such perverted joy?

When you hear that someone whom you dislike is in difficulty or is enjoying unexpected prosperity, you take the news home and mull it over when you are alone. Watch how you react. You won't feel unhappy or angry if their good fortune causes you no displeasure.

The intention of this inner debate using logic and reason is to persuade ourselves that in all circumstances anger is an inappropriate reaction. Each time we say, "But surely in this situation anger is justified," we introduce new arguments to show that it is not. Those who reject the validity of analytical meditation forgo this powerful tool for countering anger, since it requires examination of one's motives and responses and it uses a dialectic technique. They can only try to suppress all thoughts.

Concentration is not limited to the practice of placement meditation. Analytical meditation, too, requires the development of intense clarity and strong stability. Both kinds of meditation are essential if we are to overcome our inner impediments. Just as a good speaker sticks to the topic and does not ramble on about irrelevant matters, in analytical meditation discursive thought is limited to the topic under consideration and is not permitted to range freely.

From these arguments demonstrating the inappropriateness of anger, choose those that you find effective and use them in your analytical meditation. Their variety may at first seem rather overwhelming and unnecessary, but since the perfection of patience is a Bodhisattva practice, a multitude of approaches is presented. The more fuel, the stronger the fire blazes. The more approaches employed, the richer and stronger the practice of patience becomes.

We have identified the patience which takes no account of the one who harms, considered how to cultivate it, how to deal with anger, how to develop equanimity in the face of praise and blame and other potentially disturbing situations, and how to stop feelings of pleasure and displeasure at our enemies' misfortune and prosperity. Understanding these points and practicing accordingly fosters patience.

Even if we gain the ability to remain calm with those who harm us directly or indirectly, how are we to bear the difficulties and suffering that nevertheless continue to arise? How do we turn them into an adornment and squeeze some goodness out of them? In *Engaging in the Bodhisattva Deeds* Shantideva says:

> Causes for happiness are intermittent
> And there are many more causes of pain.
> Without pain there is no wish for liberation,
> Therefore, mind, remain firm.

The conditions that promote happiness are few and far between, while those that produce suffering are ever-present. Cyclic existence is full of suffering—the suffering of pain, of change and the pervasive suffering of conditioning. Unless you are willing to face this, you will never develop the wish to be free. If you can accept and cope with suffering calmly without getting upset, you can turn it into a spiritual path. If not, you will feel anger, hatred, frustration and discouragement and these emotions will act as an obstacle not only to developing higher insights but even to the most basic practice of virtue.

Some suffering is clearly inflicted by others, some needs no special precipitating circumstances and is simply the outcome of past actions, other kinds occur only when you try to practice virtue and cease as soon as you stop. When past actions yield their results, often very little can be done to stop the suffering. An ability to regard it as an adornment is essential. If you do not struggle against it, you only have the actual difficulty to deal with, which is decreased by making constructive use of it.

How is this done? Past negative actions can only come to an end in two ways: either you purify them before they ripen or you experience their consequences. When others harm you intentionally or unintentionally, when you are unhappy or in pain, try not to feel upset, but do what you can to stop the suffering and if it is unavoidable, accept it willingly. Remember that it is the consequence of your own past negative actions and that through the kindness of the Buddhas and your spiritual teachers this experience will act as a catalyst bringing to an end the negative momentum set in motion by those actions. Make the wish that it may replace the suffering of others and pray for the ocean of suffering in which living beings are drowning to dry up. If you are trying to practice virtue, think that through the force of your practice, past negative actions have come to fruition in this relatively mild human suffering instead of in a bad rebirth.

When your fortunes decline, remember that property and wealth entail many problems associated with acquiring and safeguarding them. If you own a sheep, you have a sheep's worth of worries. If you own an elephant, you have an elephant's worth! To have less means fewer worries and fewer obstacles to practicing the teachings, provided you cultivate contentment.

To develop willing acceptance of hardships, reflect on the drawbacks of happiness and the advantages of suffering. Happiness frequently leads to excitement and to disturbing emotions, especially craving, while unhappiness is a reminder to avoid non-virtue. Happiness is the result of virtue and positive energy, which will run out unless you create fresh stores. Dedicate happiness and the virtue that caused it for the good of all living beings. Dedicating it means not clinging to it selfishly but sharing it. If you do not have a good character, praise makes you conceited and arrogant. Criticism, though unpleasant to hear, helps you to identify your faults.

Contemplating these different points can help one to develop a more balanced attitude. Recognizing the dangers of happiness and the benefits of suffering is relevant to all three scopes of practice. If one is trying to gain insights in accordance with the practices of those of least capacity, understanding the futility of preoccupation with the fleeting happiness of this life is essential. It makes sense to sacrifice what is less meaningful for what is of long-term and thus of greater importance—the well-being of future lives. This involves taking sincere refuge, thinking about the connection between actions and their effects and about what should be cultivated and what discarded. Avoiding and purifying negative actions and creating virtue involves hardship. If you can accept this willingly and see it as an adornment, it will have profound implications for your future well-being.

The so-called happiness of good rebirths is spoiled by difficulties and suffering. Since it is contaminated happiness, it is unstable, untrustworthy and leads to more suffering. Seeing the drawbacks of such happiness, train yourself in ethical discipline, concentration and wisdom to gain freedom from cyclic existence. Without willingly accepting the hardships this entails you cannot gain freedom. The suffering you experience is not some punishment that has been imposed on you, but the natural consequence of your actions.

Even the happiness of personal liberation still holds pitfalls. As long as you fail to recognize the many disadvantages of self-concern you cannot truly cherish others. Without cherishing others you cannot generate the altruistic intention nor be a true practitioner of the Great Vehicle. To reach enlightenment for the sake of all living beings you must practice the six perfections. This involves many hardships. How can you hope to perfect generosity, ethics, patience, enthusiastic effort, concentration and wisdom without willingly accepting difficulties? Seeing hardships as an adornment is to see them as an opportunity and an asset. If you begin by willingly accepting minor hardships, your capacity will gradually increase.

It is sensible to accept relatively minor difficulties in order to prevent intense suffering later. Recognizing that it is possible to mine some gold from unavoidable suffering stimulates us to practice. The Buddha first pointed out our suffering, then indicated its causes and demonstrated how we can free ourselves. Thinking about the various kinds of misery that we experience arouses the wish for freedom and spurs us on towards liberation.

Suffering demonstrates to what extent we are governed by contaminated actions underlain by disturbing emotions. It deflates our pride and arrogance, which are obstructions to gaining insights. Our strong instinctive wish not to suffer reminds us that we must avoid creating the causes for suffering. This makes us take care not to act harmfully and increases our sense of self-respect and decency. If we want happiness we must set up the conditions for it. Thus suffering can encourage us in the practice of virtue. We have always been in cyclic existence and have experienced limitless suffering, including that of birth, ageing, sickness and death, time and time again. When we contemplate the fact that others are in the same predicament, empathy and compassion arise.

We have willingly put up with untold hardships in our futile search for pleasure through the objects of the five senses, but it has brought nothing of lasting value to us or others.

True wisdom lies in willingly accepting the hardships involved in doing what is meaningful and of benefit to ourselves and others. When we feel physically or mentally tired as a result of this, we should remember that such behavior befits us and is a worthwhile way of fulfilling our human potential.

It is possible to regard suffering as happiness. If we willingly accept difficulties, each hardship we face will simply increase our courage. If we lack courage, never mind our own, even others' illnesses and troubles will frighten us. When they cut themselves while cooking, people generally lose about the same amount of blood, but one person copes with this small accident calmly, while another makes a big fuss. Courage helps us to live longer because we are not in a constant state of anxiety!

Just as day is followed by night and night by day there are good times and bad times. When times are bad, take courage and think that the suffering will not last forever. When things are going well, don't be too attached to this fleeting happiness. Remember that difficulties are bound to occur again. Only by attaining liberation and enlightenment can we live in the sun all the time.

Some suffering occurs when we try to practice virtue but ceases as soon as we stop. For those living a celibate life as an ordained person, the basic requirements are an ordained person's robes, alms, a mattress, a meditation seat and medicine. When what we receive is of poor quality, too little, condescendingly or not promptly given, we should not feel displeased or upset but accept these hardships willingly. This provides us with the opportunity to cultivate contentment and few desires and to adopt a life-style that accords with the disposition of exalted beings, who are content to live on alms, wear the three robes of an ordained person, sleep on a simple mattress and who take joy in meditation and in the elimination of the disturbing emotions and of faults which need to be discarded.

As an ordained person one is supposed to shave one's head and facial hair and wear unattractive clothes with many patches. This looks ugly by ordinary standards, but we should willingly accept the hardships involved in giving up everything associated with a conventional life-style because of the benefit it brings us and others when we practice sincerely.

Those who help you cannot contribute to your development of patience, while those who harm you unintentionally assist in the process. Therefore respect them as much as enlightened beings, give them gifts and, far from being angry with them, try to help them. Enlightened and ordinary beings are equally precious as fields in which to plant the seed of everything good you desire.

Many great practitioners of the past gained perfection by devoting themselves to the happiness of others. Though the qualities possessed by the enlightened ones and by ordinary living beings are very different, both are worthy of our veneration because we gain enlightenment through our relationship to both of them. A mother is happy when we are kind to her beloved child. There is no better way of pleasing Buddhas, for whom all creatures are like beloved children, than by caring for and bringing happiness to living beings. By helping them we indirectly help ourselves and by harming them we harm ourselves. The practice of non-violence is impossible without patience.

Patiently gaining certainty with regard to the teachings entails hearing the words, taking in their meaning, thinking about it till you gain a sense of certainty and then integrating what you have understood into your life by contemplating it over and over again. This form of patience and the willing acceptance of hardship can be practiced anywhere at any time. Formal aspects of practice, such as sitting in a good meditation position with awareness of the benefits this brings, persevering with practices you have promised to do daily when you do not feel like it, or learning texts by heart involve both kinds of patience.

The patience of gaining certainty with regard to our objects of faith is developed by learning about the physical, verbal and mental qualities of enlightened beings and developing appreciation, conviction and aspiration with regard to them. The patience of gaining certainty with regard to objects that are to be directly perceived first involves an intellectual understanding of the selflessness of persons and of other phenomena. That understanding is cultivated and deepened until it becomes a direct perception.

If you like and value the teachings, your physical and verbal behavior will express your faith and respect for the Buddha from whom they originate and for those who pass the teachings on to you. You will revere the books that contain the teachings and not treat them as you might a trashy novel.

Once while I was living in West Bengal, when we first came into exile from Tibet, a friend of mine had to take an important text to a distinguished old abbot. When he reached the door, the old man motioned him to wait, rose to his feet, lit a stick of incense and with great dignity ceremonially escorted the text into the room. He then reverently placed it on a shelf and made three prostrations to it. My friend was taken aback and most impressed by such veneration.

In Tibet when the word of the Victorious One, the collection of the Buddha's sutras, was brought into a monastery, the monks, wearing their yellow robes, lined up to welcome it with incense, horns, trumpets and much pomp and circumstance. When the crops were ripening, the farmers would invite a procession of monks to carry a set of the sutras from the local monastery around the perimeter of their fields for protection.

If there was danger of a river overflowing its banks, monks would sit nearby and read from the sutras. Though this did not always stop the river from flooding, it frequently helped to mitigate the effects. People had faith in the power of truth and the power of enlightened body, speech and mind. Through their conviction extraordinary things happened.

Statues are not enlightened beings nor are the texts actually the Buddha's words, but to regard them as such brings us great benefit. If we desecrate or destroy the statues and burn the books, it doesn't hurt the enlightened ones but harms us.

Human beings want happiness. Many factors contribute to this, but one important source of happiness is to have what we need, which is the result of practicing generosity. We also must have a strong body and mind to use and enjoy the fruits of our generosity. Ethical discipline of body, speech and mind leads to this. Through generosity and ethical discipline we create much positive energy, but patience is needed to safeguard it from anger's destructive power. The Buddha's intention was to show living beings how to find happiness not how to form some kind of exclusive club. All of us can use his precious advice.

In his *Summary of the Stages of the Path* Je Tsongkhapa praises patience, saying:

> Patience is the finest adornment of the powerful,
> The best austerity to scourge the disturbing emotions.
> It is the Garuda,[19] the snake of anger's enemy,
> And a hard shield against the weapons of harsh language.
> Knowing this, grow accustomed in every way
> To the stout armor of supreme patience.

Chapter Four
Enthusiastic Effort

Enlightenment is certainly possible for those prepared to put enthusiastic effort into the practice of Bodhisattva deeds. The two great stores of merit and insight necessary for enlightenment cannot be created without such enthusiastic effort. In fact every kind of well-being to which we aspire in this and future lives depends on joyful effort. If things could be achieved by laziness, its opposite, we would have achieved all our aims long ago.

Enthusiastic effort is a delight in virtue. It is not an enthusiasm for unwholesome activities to which we often devote much effort, nor is it merely dutiful exertion to create virtue despite an innate reluctance. When true delight and enthusiasm are present, stress and weariness do not occur.

There are three main types of enthusiastic effort: armor-like enthusiastic effort, enthusiastic effort in the creation of virtue and enthusiastic effort in working for others.[20]

Armor-like enthusiastic effort consists of being prepared to do as much, go as deeply and continue for as long as is necessary to achieve a positive objective. With it we would be prepared to spend a lifetime, even aeons, in a hell rebirth and put up with every difficulty to help a single being. Lacking it, we are impatient and want to attain our objectives in as short a time and with as little effort as possible. Such an attitude is an obstacle to the Bodhisattva way of life and an indication that it will take a long time to reach enlightenment. Armor-like enthusiastic effort speeds us on our way.

Enthusiastic effort in creating virtue is a delight in the practice of the six perfections. Enthusiastic effort in working for living beings entails wholeheartedly devoting our physical energy and resources to helping them and joyfully engaging in the eleven ways of working for them, which have already been discussed.

In his *Three Principal Aspects of the Path*[21] Je Tsongkhapa says:

> Child, when you have properly understood
> The important points of the three principal paths,
> Seek seclusion and with strong enthusiasm
> Quickly insure the good of all future lives.

Three forms of laziness prevent us from doing what Tsongkhapa recommends: procrastination, involvement in trivial activities and discouragement. Laziness stops us achieving anything useful and is a fertile growing medium for all the disturbing emotions. It is easy to be both extremely busy and lazy at the same time!

What causes us to delay our practice of virtue? It may be an addiction to idleness or to sleep. It may be attachment to pleasure. We delay because we do not fear bad states of rebirth and have no aversion to cyclic existence. Do any or all of these affect you? Time passes as you keep putting off what in your heart you know you must do.

We take pleasure in many kinds of trivial activities and eagerly engage in them. Almost everything we enjoy falls into this category. The sense of achievement and fame from strenuous and dangerous activities such as mountaineering or sailing around the world single-handedly brings some short-lived happiness, but they are of no lasting benefit to oneself or others and are said to be trivial, even bad, since from a different perspective they are a waste of our human potential.

We feel discouraged by the extensiveness of the practices and deterred by the difficulty of understanding the philosophy that underlies them, but in fact our remarkable physical and mental stamina allows us to do and understand anything we wish. This is our greatest treasure and resource. Is the true meaning of our human life just to look after friends and loved ones and to crush our enemies? Do we fulfill our human potential by vying with and preying on each other? Instead we can throw off the laziness which impedes us, use our intelligence to rid ourselves of the despotic disturbing emotions and allow true kindness to grow in our hearts. We know this but are reluctant to let it change our lives. Shantideva says:

> This freedom and fortune are very hard to find.
> Having gained what can accomplish a living being's aims,
> If I do not use it well now,
> How shall I meet with such goodness later?

He reminds us that if we make effort, while we have the freedom and fortune we enjoy at present, we can certainly free ourselves from suffering, so we must use the ship of our precious human rebirth to cross the wild ocean of cyclic existence.

A precious human life such as this is rare and special. We are free from eight adverse conditions. Four of these are non-human states as hell-beings, animals, hungry ghosts and celestial beings with extremely long lives. The suffering of those in the bad states of rebirth is so intense that they cannot think about spiritual practice. Celestial beings with long lives are absorbed in sensual pleasures or the pleasure of concentration and cannot develop an aversion to cyclic existence. Their bodies and minds are not suitable as a basis for vows of any kind.

There are four human states which prevent spiritual practice, the most serious of which is holding wrong views such as that there are no past and future lives and that there is no connection between actions and their effects. Being born a barbarian in a remote place where there is no access to Buddhist teachings, being born at a time when a Buddha's teachings do not exist in the world and having defective faculties are also serious impediments.

Fortune means enjoying conducive conditions. Five kinds of such fortune are personal: being born as a human; being born in a place where the teachings exist and there are ordained men and women; possessing healthy faculties; not having created any seriously negative actions like the five extremely grave and the five almost as grave actions;[22] and having faith in spiritual teachers, the three kinds of training and the texts which contain instructions on them. Five kinds of good fortune are circumstantial: that a Buddha has come to the world; that he has lit the lamp of the teachings; that these teachings are alive insofar as there are people who hear, think about and meditate on them; that there are those who can be looked upon as role-models because of their exemplary practice of the teachings; and that support and encouragement for practitioners is available.

It is irrelevant how many human beings there are in the world because a human rebirth of leisure and fortune remains rare as long as we have not created the excellent virtue which gives rise to it. If we have, we are assured of a good human life. You don't need an astrological chart or a divination to know what kind of rebirth lies ahead. Just look into your heart and mind.

Of all the people in the world how many have heard the Buddha's teachings? And of those who have, how many have a genuine desire to put them into practice? How many of those who wish to practice have the opportunity to do so? The strong virtue and positive energy needed to create such a situation come about through the practice of ethics, patience and generosity.

Anyone with a real conviction that harmful actions bring suffering and wholesome ones bring happiness will make concerted effort to discard destructive conduct and foster constructive thoughts and behavior. The peaceful path of non-violence consists of restraint from detrimental physical and verbal actions and is based on non-attachment, lack of anger and lack of confusion. To follow this path one needs to understand well what constitutes violence and non-violence and what their results are. The practice of non-violence is the quintessence of Buddhism and whoever lives it, turning away from harmful actions and encouraging others to do likewise, is a true practitioner and a good human being. Make your life worthwhile before it is too late. Your present fortunate situation can change at any moment. Death is never more than a breath away and after death you must take a new rebirth, in which you may not enjoy the same opportunities.

To develop enthusiastic effort you must overcome laziness by discovering and stopping its causes. Both types of meditation, analytical and placement, are used in most meditation practices, such as counteracting the disturbing emotions, contemplating the marvelous qualities of enlightened body, speech and mind or cultivating love and compassion. Having prepared the room and sat down on your meditation cushion, put on your armor of enthusiastic effort. Creating the intention to concentrate on the focal object without any distraction for the whole session, no matter which kind of meditation you employ, is to put on the armor of enthusiastic effort. Protected by it you ward off drowsiness and lethargy. When you feel sleepy or tempted to postpone your practice, remember the old don't necessarily die first and the young later. Think about anything which inspires you with a sense of urgency, until the enthusiasm to practice arises.

Everything the Buddha taught, both the sutras and tantras, is for meditation and for practical application. The survival of his teachings is endangered when people think the sutras and tantras are for recitation or for oral transmission and what is to be practiced in meditation must be sought elsewhere. The Buddha's teaching is worth keeping alive because of the benefits its practice bestows on us and others. No wiser, more compassionate teacher nor any greater practitioner than the Buddha can be found, which is not to say that there are no other wise, compassionate or great teachers! If we practice sincerely what the founder of any authentic spiritual tradition has taught, it will bring us and others much good.

Even if we succeed in overcoming the tendency to delay, we may still be attached to the pleasure of trivial activities and amusements. Since these are the only joys and pleasures we know, it isn't surprising that such activities enthrall us. Though they are undeniably enjoyable, they prevent the practice of what can bring us supreme happiness and our attachment to these activities often leads to unwholesome actions which result in suffering. We love talking but find talk of virtue boring. We prefer spicy conversation which arouses desire, envy, competitiveness or hostility. Since we have studied and practiced only a little, we have never really tasted the teachings. Once we savor their incomparable taste, nothing else will ever be as flavorful, virtue will never again seem boring and enthusiastic effort will come naturally.

"Trivial activities" refers to anything done for respect or reward, most kinds of busyness, meaningless conversation, unwholesome pursuits and even enterprises like farming or commerce when done with attachment. Though such ordinary work is not unwholesome in itself, it is considered trivial in that it usually prevents the development of any powerful spiritual attainments. Effort and enthusiasm directed towards any of these occupations is not the enthusiastic effort of delight in virtue. When tempted by meaningless distractions, remember that practicing the teachings brings boundless joy in this and future lives. Why turn your back on true happiness and waste your energy on pursuits which prevent you doing anything really meaningful in this life and which easily become a cause for future suffering? An intelligent person willingly sacrifices what is of lesser value.

You may wonder whether from a Buddhist point of view every kind of artistic endeavor necessarily falls into this category. Consider these two examples. A musician with the strong wish to bring joy and pleasure to others, not just humans but even to animals, spends much time practicing and perfecting his or her art. Another person, a scholar of Buddhism, enthusiastically and assiduously does years of research on great texts with the intention of writing a book, becoming famous and making a lot of money. Who is practicing true enthusiastic effort? Motivation determines the ultimate worth of any activity.

The causes that give rise to happiness are called virtue and those that give rise to unhappiness, non-virtue. Happiness comes from states of mind which are peaceful and disciplined. Once your mind is more peaceful, your physical and verbal activity will also undergo a positive change. You will avoid harming others, stop feeling discontent and create the causes for future well-being. All the favorable conditions for bringing about these changes are present.

You may resolve to make best use of these circumstances while they last, overcome attachment to trivial activities and develop a genuine interest in what the Buddha taught, but now the daunting task of implementing the many profound and extensive practices of the Great Vehicle lies ahead. A magnificent result such as enlightenment, the complete elimination of all faults and perfection of all good qualities, can only result from the creation of equally significant causes. If one is unaware of what must be overcome and developed on the path, this prospect will not fill one with awe.

If one understands the immensity of this undertaking—complete enlightenment for the sake of all living beings in order to relieve their suffering and bring them happiness—

one may feel disheartened. We have vowed to rid ourselves of all faults, overcome all limitations and fully develop our human potential. This may seem overwhelming when we consider how hard it is to get rid of even a single bad habit or to develop a new accomplishment.

Discouraged, we may think, "How can I ever attain enlightenment if this is what's involved?" But armored with the right kind of enthusiasm we will gladly spend a whole lifetime just learning to appreciate fully the preciousness of our human rebirth. When we have endured all kinds of meaningless hardships in the past, surely it is worth enduring difficulties for this great purpose.

The Buddha, whose words are trustworthy, said all living beings from the smallest insect have the ability to become enlightened. This statement can be substantiated by reasoning and need not be accepted simply because it was made by the Buddha. The clear-light nature of the mind endows every being with the potential to be totally free from stains and to develop every kind of good quality. The disturbing emotions are temporary and can be got rid of through the application of antidotes. By learning, reflecting and integrating the teachings through meditation we can develop our capabilities. All beings are the same in this, so where does the difference lie? In whether we are able to make enthusiastic effort or not.

Once the Buddha, in whom we now take refuge, was exactly like us, but through his own efforts he became enlightened and then taught from his personal experience. There is no reason to feel inferior, for we too can become enlightened in the same way. Moreover, if it is true that all living beings have the potential to become enlightened, we as humans enjoy a special advantage because of our superior intelligence, which allows us to discriminate clearly between what needs to be cultivated and what needs to be discarded. Therefore feel encouraged and think, "Why shouldn't I reach enlightenment?"

The whole question of our human potential and the nature of mind is something worth taking time to contemplate and study. Only then will you gain any sense of conviction regarding your true capabilities. You will find that the premises on which the Buddha's teachings are based do not fall apart but can withstand scrutiny. The deeper you delve, the more convincing they become. If on investigation something becomes clearer and clearer, not fuzzier and fuzzier, and if many plausible reasons seem to support it, then even if you have not yet gained certainty, it is sensible to accept it for the time being.

Instead of turning your attention outward, look within to discover the true and amazing nature of your body and mind. During twenty-four hours both undergo constant change and pass through coarse and subtle states. It is worth examining the various kinds of awareness which manifest as you dream, during deep sleep and when you awake, particularly because of their relation to death, the intermediate state and rebirth.

Do you ever think about these things? Do you ever wonder whether the dream person exists? What do you say when your child asks, "Where did I come from?" Do you point to your belly and say, "From here"? And what if the child inquires, "How did I get there?" Will you give a purely physiological explanation or answer, "I don't know"?

In the *Sutra Encouraging the Special Wish*[23] the Buddha says:

> Enthusiastic effort praised by all Buddhas is transcendent.
> It removes all suffering and darkness
> And is the basis for completely ending bad rebirths,
> So cultivate it continually.
> Those who make enthusiastic effort
> Will have no difficulty accomplishing
> Every worldly and supramundane art.
> What wise person with strong enthusiasm is discouraged?
> Those engaged in attaining enlightenment,
> Seeing the drawbacks of lethargy and sleepiness,
> Spend their time making constant enthusiastic effort.
> I have encouraged them in this.

The eccentric Tibetan practitioner Drukpa Kunlek[24] once went on pilgrimage to see the famous statue of the Buddha called "the Lord"[25] in the main temple in Lhasa. When he finally stood before the statue, he addressed it, saying, "Once you and I were the same, but you made effort and became enlightened and I'm still in this condition because of my laziness, which is why I'm obliged to pay homage to you now," and he made prostrations to the Buddha.

In the past in Tibet there were people who hoped, and still now there are those who hope, to attain enlightenment by concentrating on a single practice, such as attempting to stop all thought or holding the energy winds in a particular formation. How can a single limited practice produce a result as magnificent as enlightenment?

When someone describes the principles of archery it seems easy enough, but when you pick up the bow and arrow yourself, you understand how difficult it is. You don't realize what is involved in a new discipline until you begin, and at that point you may well feel discouraged. You may wonder, "How could I ever develop the altruistic intention or practice generosity the way a Bodhisattva does, if I have to be prepared to give even parts of my body?"

In fact you have borne far greater suffering for no good purpose at all during innumerable past lifetimes in cyclic existence. Your head and limbs have been chopped off, you have been beaten, cut, pierced and tormented in every way imaginable. Even if you disregard the suffering you have endured in bad rebirths, think about the different kinds of mutilation you have endured as a human in past lives. Can any of us be certain that we have never experienced such suffering or that we will never experience it again? The hardship of practicing is relatively small by comparison. Though this is so, it means little to us because our belief in rebirth is at best superficial.

Even if you recognize the truth of this, you may feel very frightened of having to give away your limbs, but this is not necessary at present. Begin by giving what is easy, such as water, flowers, food or clothing. As attachment to your body decreases and your courage and compassion grow, your capacity to give will increase until you are able to give your limbs easily without experiencing any distress. In this way you become capable of practicing the inconceivable deeds of the Great Vehicle without feeling it is a sacrifice. The Buddha taught the easy path to a great result. He did not recommend extreme ascetic practices but the middle way of moderation in all things.

Once a great master was asked for teaching on the correct view of reality. He praised the request, but said it would be more beneficial to teach the whole path to enlightenment, which, of course, includes discussion of the correct view. Why was he insistent on this? It is important to insure that your understanding and practice are not partial. Every day try to do a scanning meditation of all the aspects of practice necessary for the attainment of enlightenment and then concentrate your effort on the area in which you are trying to gain insights. Even if you do not attain any profound realizations, you will at least have established imprints for the complete path by doing this. If, on the other hand, you don't do such a review in meditation but employ only a specific meditation technique and fail to gain the desired results, you will not have established those precious predispositions either. Each time you sit down to meditate, know what you intend to do and the steps you intend to follow. Your practice should be a complete one. Then, in each session, spend as long or as little time as you wish on the different parts of your practice.

You may overcome discouragement and recognize that enlightenment can be achieved. You may also stop feeling disheartened by the difficulty of the practices which make this possible because you realize the process of training is gradual. But you may still feel daunted by the length of time all this will take and by the prospect of enduring suffering in cyclic existence for so long. However there are ways to remain in cyclic existence without experiencing physical and mental suffering. If you are happy, what does it matter how long you remain here? If you are suffering, even a minute is too long.

While you have this contaminated body and mind, the result of actions underlain by disturbing attitudes and emotions, you are fettered to suffering. Even if you aren't experiencing outright suffering, it can flare up at any moment. You therefore lack freedom and cannot avoid suffering at present. You are forced to go where your contaminated actions propel you and you are ruled by turbulent emotions, an implacable enemy. This is the situation of living beings as long as they remain in cyclic existence.

The situation of Bodhisattvas is different. The fact that their actions are not polluted by negative mental states frees them from the causes of physical suffering. Most of our suffering stems from our fixed ideas and ways of thinking. Since Bodhisattvas understand the nature of reality, they do not cling to ideas of a truly existent self, body or mind, which frees them from the causes of mental suffering. They therefore do not experience suffering, no matter how long they remain in the world.

Although enormous stores of positive energy and insight are needed for the attainment of enlightenment, there are skillful ways of creating them rapidly. When we devote ourselves wholeheartedly to the happiness of living beings as limitless as space and take the Bodhisattva vow for this purpose, whether we make conscious effort or not, positive energy accumulates day and night as long as our vow remains intact. This is how merit that would otherwise take aeons to accumulate is rapidly created. Virtuous actions done by someone holding any of the vows—the refuge vow, lay-person's vows, Bodhisattva or tantric vows—become more powerful than they would ordinarily be. This is one reason why holding such vows is considered of great value.

If you are not content merely with making your physical and verbal actions peaceful and controlled, but with all your heart seek to relieve the suffering of others and out of such compassion and love intensely and urgently wish to attain enlightenment, the swift methods of the tantric path are available to you. But if you are simply looking for a short-cut because you are discouraged by the task that lies ahead and the length of time it will require, the tantric path is not for you.

Having understood how to overcome the obstacles which hinder you from developing, sustaining and enhancing enthusiastic effort, consider the factors that support it. Mindfulness, alertness and care lead to spontaneous enthusiastic effort in anything virtuous you choose to undertake. Four forces contribute to this: a belief in the value of virtue and the aspiration to practice it gives you the impetus to develop enthusiastic effort. Constancy enables you to persevere and enthusiastically follow through with what you have begun. Joy allows you to do it with the delight of a child at play, while knowing when to relax permits you to stop when you feel tired and begin again with renewed energy when you are rested.

The object of your aspiration is the cultivation of what needs to be developed and the elimination of what needs to be discarded. Such aspiration is the wellspring for enthusiastic effort and in this context comes from thinking about the great benefits of practicing the six perfections and the drawbacks of not doing so.

Why does aspiration play an important role? We have never really had the wish to rid ourselves of unwholesome thoughts and actions nor to cultivate wholesome ones. This is why we have continued to wander in cyclic existence, constantly experiencing troubles and miseries. Every intelligent person longs for freedom and happiness. When we think sufficiently about the fruition of actions—how white or constructive actions produce agreeable experiences and black or harmful actions produce disagreeable ones, we will gain a sense of conviction and certainty. This leads to aspiration, which in turn gives rise to enthusiastic effort.

If we are genuinely interested in the Great Vehicle and wish to practice accordingly, we must first develop the altruistic intention and try to purify faults and their imprints as well as help others to do so. This is what we promise to do when we take the Bodhisattva vow. Is our enthusiasm sufficient to apply the necessary antidotes to our selfish impulses for as long as is needed to overcome them? If we continue to be halfhearted and apathetic in our attempts, we will create more negative actions that will force us to experience further suffering. The thought of this should break our hearts, but it doesn't because our hearts are hard and we lack compassion even towards ourselves.

When we take the Bodhisattva vow, we commit ourselves to magnificent deeds of virtue. Without enthusiastic effort none of these are possible. Since we don't know what our next rebirth will be like, it is imperative to make good our promise, while we have the use of our strong human body and mind.

Do we give gifts to those in whom we take refuge and please them in other ways? Do we provide feasts of joy for living beings? Do we make them happy by offering them our respect and service? Do we implement the teachings by avoiding wrong-doing and engaging in virtue? Do we rescue and protect those in fear and danger? Do we satisfy the needy with food and clothing? What do we do for living beings?

If we do none of this, what purpose has our birth from the womb served other than to give our mother pain? We have reason to regret. If we have done good in our lives, we should allow it to give us joy and inspire us to do more. When we honestly consider our actions and take the tally, we will come to know ourselves.

Sometimes it is useful to reflect on what you have done right because that serves as an encouragement. The fact that you are able to stand on your own feet in the world and are a decent person is because, generally speaking, you followed your parents' and teachers' advice. This is the most basic practice of cultivating what is constructive and discarding what is not. We see what happens when others don't do it. An assertion of independence can go very wrong.

In developing the positive and discarding the negative, constancy enables you to make unremitting effort. Before undertaking anything examine whether it is an appropriate course of action or not. Even if it is, you must consider whether or not you are capable of it. It is better not to begin something than to begin and abandon it halfway through. This can lead to the bad habit of taking up one thing after another and never completing anything. Such a pattern prevents you from honoring commitments and creating fresh virtue. It also robs you of satisfaction.

Three kinds of pride are cultivated to further constancy. With the pride of action you resolve to act without hoping for or depending on anyone else's help. In his *Letter to a Friend* Nagarjuna says:

> Liberation depends on yourself and in this
> Nobody else can assist you. Those who have heard,
> Have ethical discipline and concentration
> Should make effort in the four truths.

Liberation is freedom from the bondage of contaminated actions and disturbing emotions. No one can take you by the hand and lead you to that state. You must gain the necessary insights and reach that state yourself by ridding yourself of suffering and its causes. After dinner no one feels like moving and everyone waits for someone else to get up and clear the table. If you make the first move, others may decide to help, but while you expect something of them, you are ill at ease and anxious. If you take the initiative to begin freeing yourself from old and harmful emotional habits and attitudes, the support you need will come.

Most people are so much under the influence of disturbing emotions that they cannot even look after themselves let alone others. Recognizing the extent to which they are engrossed in trivial worldly concerns and mindful of your promise to alleviate suffering and give happiness, accept personal responsibility when performing any action intended to benefit others. Motivated by genuine compassion do this with no feelings of superiority but with confident pride in your abilities.

Finally there is pride in the face of the disturbing emotions. Counter them with the determination that you will not let them get the better of you but will valiantly resist and overcome their tyranny. If you lack such fierce determination and are faint-hearted, the slightest setback will turn into a major obstacle.

A crow acts as brave as a garuda when faced with a dead snake but doesn't dare to go near a live one. You must develop strong counteractions to the disturbing emotions. Those who combat them are truly heroic, not those who swagger about puffed up with pride when they are actually enslaved by their enemy.

Joy consists of continuing what you have undertaken with the delight of a child engrossed in play. A child's enjoyment of what it is doing is so great that it cannot bear to stop. Relaxing or stopping at the right moment permits you to rest before you are totally exhausted. If you continue till your mental or physical strength runs out, your task will seem overwhelming and you will feel nauseated by the mere thought of what remains to be done. If you take a rest, you will be better able to continue with renewed vigor. When you have completed one thing, allow yourself to catch your breath before beginning something new.

Especially when you are engaged in stressful work such as nursing the sick, it is vital to rest before you feel completely depleted. If you wait too long, you will be forced to rest anyway and instead of one sick person there will be two. Sometimes, when your presence for an extra few minutes or hours will make a significant difference, you must put the other person's needs first. However, it is important to become skillful in managing your own resources of energy.

Aspiration, stability, joy and taking a rest reinforce enthusiastic effort and help it to grow. Encouraging others to develop greater enthusiasm for worthwhile activities is a form of generosity.

We have considered the benefits of enthusiastic effort and the disadvantages of laziness, what constitutes enthusiastic effort, its various forms, different manifestations of laziness, how to combat them and how to support and enhance enthusiastic effort. Mental and physical pliancy are the ultimate antidote to laziness. Thinking about our impending death counteracts our tendency to delay. Considering the preciousness of our life and the difficulty of finding such a rare situation of freedom and fortune curtails our involvement in trivial activities. Fully recognizing the conducive inner and outer circumstances we enjoy and our freedom from obstacles helps to overcome discouragement.

Which kind of laziness do you suffer from? Some people just like to be idle and put things off. Some are very busy and pursue a great variety of interests. Some don't realize how strong their body and mind are and suffer from feelings of inferiority. As soon as we tackle one kind of laziness, another suddenly appears to be more prominent, but this is merely because we have begun to pay attention to our mental and physical habits.

In his Summary of the *Stages of the Path* Je Tsongkhapa encourages us to develop the ability to make enthusiastic effort by saying:

> Armored with unremitting and steady effort,
> Scriptural knowledge and insight grow like the
>   waxing moon.
> All your activities become meaningful
> And whatever you undertake you will complete
>   successfully.
> Knowing this Bodhisattvas exert themselves
> To make powerful enthusiastic effort
> Which dispels all laziness.

Chapter Five
Concentration

Once strong enthusiastic effort has been developed it must be applied to the cultivation of meditative stabilization, because while slackness and excitement influence our mind, the disturbing emotions can like carnivorous beasts attack and devour us. Shantideva says:

> Thus having developed enthusiastic effort,
> Place your mind in meditative stabilization.
> People whose minds are distracted
> Live between the fangs of the disturbing emotions.

Both Buddhists and non-Buddhists cultivate meditative stabilization. The eight concentrations of the form and formless realms[26] are also mentioned in non-Buddhist literature. When meditative stabilization is practiced with sincere refuge in the Three Jewels, it is a Buddhist practice. When practiced with an understanding of the disadvantages of cyclic existence and a wish to gain freedom, it becomes a cause for liberation. Without a calmly abiding mind it is impossible to achieve the states of meditative stabilization described in sutra or to accomplish the stages of generation and completion of tantra.[27] In fact it acts as a vessel for all higher realizations, just as a container is needed for collecting water. The achievement of concentration is not an end in itself. It is a key which opens the door to many different practices. Most important, it is used to gain a profound understanding of reality.

Since cyclic existence is synonymous with suffering, the only way to rid ourselves of suffering is to gain freedom from cyclic existence. The ignorance that lies at its root cannot be eradicated except by gaining special insight into the nature of reality. Such special insight is unattainable without the development of a calmly abiding mind. Emptiness can be understood without it, but if the understanding is to be sufficiently powerful, it must be both clear and stable, just as a clear and steady light is needed to see the details of a wall-painting in a dark room.

Reality, the selflessness of persons and other phenomena, is like a form to be seen, and understanding is like the eye. If the form is too distant from the eye, it can't be seen clearly, but when a steady hand is used to bring the form close, every detail can be perceived. A calmly abiding mind is like the steady hand.

As we develop a calmly abiding mind, inner distractions are overcome, but first we must be free from the coarse external distractions created by unwholesome physical and verbal activities. An essential foundation for developing a calmly abiding mind is the observance of ethical discipline, specifically restraint from the ten harmful activities. Buddhist practice consists of view, meditation and conduct. View, the correct understanding of reality, is based on meditation, the practice of concentration. The basis for both is ethical conduct. A good practitioner places equal emphasis on all three.

With a stable mind any positive practice, such as meditation on the preciousness of our human life, on impermanence or visualization of a deity, becomes more effective and insights are gained more quickly. A calmly abiding mind is essential for the development of clairvoyance, different kinds of extrasensory perception and miraculous feats. While ethical discipline stops unwholesome physical and verbal activities, the expression of the disturbing emotions, concentration stops all manifest forms of the disturbing emotions. Special insight allows us to get rid even of their imprints.

If you want to change and aspire to see others change, if you hope for peace in the world, you must begin by making yourself more peaceful. When your friends notice a positive transformation in you, they will be curious to know what caused it and your presence will begin to inspire those around you. This is how change is set in motion and is the only way to create peace within and between nations. It is futile to dream of peace while the disturbing emotions rage within us.

Without the essential outer and inner conditions you can develop greater concentration but not a calmly abiding mind. These conditions include a suitable place, having few wishes, contentment, freedom from busyness, a wholesome life-style and lack of preoccupation with sense stimuli. Then, if you have received correct instruction and practice accordingly, you have a good chance of developing a calmly abiding mind. Without these prerequisites, you will not, no matter how long you practice.

Many people are interested in developing higher states of concentration, but if they lack an interest in creating the basic inner conditions their aspiration is meaningless. If you want the fruit, you must tend the plant and provide the right growing conditions. The root of concentration is mindfulness, the ability to retain your focal object. How mindful are you and do you work at increasing your mindfulness on and off your meditation cushion?

In his *Ornament for the Mahayana Sutras* Maitreya speaks of the ideal place for intensive practice:

> In an intelligent person's place of practice
> Things are well found, the site is good.
> The ground is good, there are good friends
> And the tools for a practitioner's happiness.

In the place you choose for meditation what is needed for daily life should be readily available and gained without wrong-doing. If, for example, food and water are not easy to come by, you will expend much time and energy procuring them, which will leave little of both for meditation. A sacred place, blessed by the presence of great practitioners in the past, is considered particularly auspicious. Such places have the power to bless one in that they inspire faith and the wish to practice.

Certainly the place should be peaceful and not one where acts of violence are known to have occurred. It should be free of danger from humans and wild animals. Some people intentionally meditate in dangerous places to show their daring, but this is unwise for any but advanced practitioners. A constant underlying anxiety will disturb one's peace of mind.

Choose a healthy place which suits your constitution. The proximity of good companions who share your views and aspirations is important, since being alone can be dangerous for a beginner and practicing among good companions is encouraging. A good companion is someone who is prepared to point out your faults, not someone who indulges you. There should be as little noise as possible from water or wild animals, since noise is one of the chief sources of distraction.

In addition equip yourself with the tools for a practitioner's happiness. Know what to practice and dispel doubts by hearing and thinking about the instructions. Become conversant with the order in which to proceed and rich in knowledge about your meditation topic. How strange if you invest much energy in assembling all the external conditions, but neglect these vital inner ones. You may end up in the ideal place without knowing what to do in meditation. Others know exactly what to do and are ready to begin but spend years looking for a suitable place. It is difficult to assemble all the inner and outer conditions.

Physical seclusion is important, but you also need to find inner quiet and seclusion from mental busyness. When you have the food, clothing and accommodation you need, cultivate contentment and don't wish for more or better facilities. The time will never come when everything is perfect. Preoccupation with accumulating, safeguarding and increasing your property is a distraction. In the end you become a servant to your possessions because greed is a hard taskmaster and makes you suffer.

Busyness sends you here and there. You spend much time talking and even when you finally sit down, you can think of nothing but plans and projects. The fewer wishes you have and the more content you are, the less busy your life becomes. When trying to develop higher concentration even studies, which under other circumstances are of benefit, act as a distraction.

An ethical life-style is essential, since the wind of unwholesome physical and verbal actions creates turbulence on the lake of the mind. The waves must die down, for when the surface is still anything can be mirrored in it. In order to deal with the subtle inner distractions, coarse external ones must first cease. Attraction to sense stimuli causes the mind to wander. You may plan to do your meditation session and afterwards some other enjoyable activity to which you look forward. Anticipation of pleasure remains present subliminally and distracts the mind during meditation.

There are five faults or problems which prevent us from gaining a calmly abiding mind. These are counteracted by eight antidotes.[28] Having created conducive conditions for the cultivation of a calmly abiding mind, you may be reluctant to begin the practice. This is the first fault and the effect of laziness, the ultimate antidote to which is complete mental and physical pliancy. But pliancy cannot be achieved without enthusiastic perseverance. Enthusiasm won't arise unless there is an aspiration to develop a calmly abiding mind, yet this will only be present if you fully appreciate the benefits a calmly abiding mind will bring. The main advantage is that it forms the basis for developing special insight into the nature of reality through which the root of our suffering can be cut. Of course, such a benefit is only meaningful to those intent on ridding themselves of suffering!

Calm abiding enables you to direct your mind where you wish and to maintain your attention on a particular focal object for as long as you desire. Such intense attention brings impressive results. Two sticks rubbed together make fire, but only when they are rubbed together continuously in the same place. Even if you are unable to develop such a high degree of mental control, greater mental stability would significantly enhance your well-being and happiness.

Anything, a stone or a flower, can serve as an object for the development of a calmly abiding mind, but it is wisest to choose something that will help you to accomplish various purposes simultaneously, such as the accumulation of positive energy and purification. An image of the Buddha or, in the context of tantra, a seed syllable[29] at one of the energy centers of the body is frequently chosen.

Sutra describes four main categories of focal objects.[30] You are not called upon to adopt them all, but only what is suitable in your particular case. A supermarket offers a wide selection of goods at different prices and of different qualities, but you don't feel compelled to buy everything on sale. You choose what you need and want.

Many different disturbing emotions affect us, but identifying and countering your predominant disturbing emotion is important, otherwise it will repeatedly interfere with your practice. You can tell if you have had much familiarity with a disturbing emotion in the past and not regarded it as a fault if a slight stimulus triggers intense emotion that lasts for a long time. When a moderate stimulus is needed and the emotion does not last long, you can infer that you did not habitually experience this emotion, but neither did you regard it as faulty. If the emotion only arises weakly in the presence of a strong stimulus and is short-lived, you can conclude that you had very little familiarity with it in past lives and considered it detrimental.

We are reluctant to scrutinize ourselves too closely or acknowledge our predominant disturbing emotion because our misconception of the self and our egocentrism, from which the three poisons and all the other disturbing emotions arise, make us defensive. But if we really seek our own well-being and cherish ourselves, we must identify that emotion and apply the appropriate counteractions. While these emotions continue to dominate us, we remain under the control of merciless foes who allow us no happiness. Fortunately, since they are not an integral part of us, it is possible to rid ourselves of their destructive influence.

In order to practice effectively you must know in theory what problems you are likely to encounter and how to counteract them. You must also learn to identify them in your own meditative experience. For instance, you must be able clearly to recognize slackness and excitement when they occur. This cannot be done without knowing their characteristics.

As mentioned above, four of the eight antidotes counteract laziness: physical and mental pliancy, enthusiastic effort, aspiration and interest in the benefits of developing a calmly abiding mind. Once you begin the practice, the next problem you encounter is "forgetting the instructions." This means that the focal object becomes extremely unclear or you lose it altogether. Without a focal object, there is nothing on which to center your attention.

The antidote to losing the object is mindfulness which is characterized by three features: its object is something already familiar; its aspect is to hold that object without forgetting it, just as the thought of food or water is constantly present in your mind when you are very hungry or thirsty; its function is to prevent the mind from being distracted to something else. Mindfulness is important not only in meditation but in daily life. If you are distracted and absentminded in the kitchen, the food gets burnt and you have to spend twice as long cleaning up the mess.

If you choose, for instance, to concentrate on an image of the Buddha, you must first familiarize yourself with it by looking at a painting or statue or by receiving detailed instruction on what to imagine. Then evoke the image as clearly as possible and focus intense and continuous attention on it.

One corner of the mind watches to see whether this is happening. Driving is a useful analogy here. The driver's main attention is on the road ahead, but at the same time he or she remains aware of what is happening behind and to the sides. For beginners the main task is simply to sustain attention on the object. As soon as mental alertness spots that things are going wrong, that the object is about to be or has been lost, effort is made to recall it. This is the basis for any further development in the practice of concentration.

In Buddhist discussion of mental activity a division is made into mind and mental factors. Mind refers to six types of consciousness, five associated with the five senses and one with the mental faculty. Mental factors or functions accompany these kinds of consciousness. One of these functions, the mind's ability to remain single-pointed, is called meditative stabilization. We all have some ability to concentrate. The mental factor enabling maintenance of concentration is mindfulness, and that which keeps watch on the process is mental alertness, an aspect of knowledge.

Although in the description of the five faults and eight antidotes mental alertness is cited as the antidote to slackness and excitement, the third of the faults, it is not the actual antidote but the mental activity which notes their occurrence. Mental alertness must be so refined that it can detect the subtlest forms of slackness and excitement, noticing them as soon as they begin.

Many of us dislike the effort involved in analytical meditation and think that placement meditation is easier and more restful. This is a misapprehension. The achievement of a calmly abiding mind, characterized by intense clarity and strong stability, demands much effort, intelligence and skill. Since slackness and excitement hinder the achievement of combined clarity and stability, they are considered the main obstacles to calm abiding.

Identifying these obstacles carefully is important, otherwise, for instance, lethargy may be mistaken for slackness when in fact it is a cause of slackness. A practitioner may think that slackness has been eliminated when, in fact, lethargy has been counteracted, and may mistake the dull stability achieved for a satisfactory state of concentration. Meanwhile the subtle slackness which is present remains unaffected.

In his *Compendium of Knowledge*[31] Asanga defines excitement as a mental state focusing on an attractive object or one which appears attractive to the mind. Excitement is an aspect of desire in the form of craving. It is never virtuous but may be unspecified or non-virtuous. It makes the mind unpeaceful and therefore obstructs calm abiding. Thinking about someone or something we dislike is distraction and one of the subsidiary disturbing emotions. Thinking about something positive may be inspiring but also acts as a distraction and an obstacle to calm abiding, although it is not distraction which involves disturbing emotions. Allowing the mind to roam freely, no matter how glorious our imaginings may be, prevents concentration because mindfulness, the root of all meditative stabilization, is absent. Since distraction can be caused by desire, hostility or confusion, why is the kind referred to as excitement singled out here? This is because the most frequently experienced distraction in meditation is caused by desire or attachment.

Safeguarding mindfulness at all times is important. Many people think one glass of alcohol doesn't matter, but even one decreases mindfulness slightly, and one drink leads to another. Lack of mindfulness is responsible for all kinds of accidents. If a small amount of a particular substance didn't have the power to decrease mindfulness slightly, how could a large amount diminish it radically?

All the emotions in the desire syndrome are hard to see as detrimental because initially when they arise they feel stimulating and pleasant, but their harmfulness is evident from the fact that they eventually bring us trouble and pain. Clinging and possessiveness create constant anxiety and prevent us from being generous even to ourselves. Craving and addiction to different pleasures injure our health and may lead to crimes for which we must bear imprisonment and in some countries physical punishments, such as amputation of one's limbs or being bound and beaten. Indeed, most crimes are motivated by desire or attachment, which manifest in many forms and bring one misery in this and future lives.

Understanding this and overcoming our clinging can only enrich us and will not impoverish us as we fear. Clinging to the self is uprooted by investigating its actual nature and by understanding that it exists, but not as we assume. Clinging to our personal happiness decreases as we realize our true connection to others and the great benefits of cherishing them. We begin to recognize that while our own happiness is important, that of other living beings, who are in the majority, is of greater importance. By contemplating the less appealing aspects of the sense objects and our responses to them, we become less attached, develop greater generosity and discover a wholesome middle way of neither depriving nor pampering ourselves. By these means we stop the causes of the excitement which acts as an obstacle to calm abiding.

The other main obstacle, slackness, makes us lose our focal object entirely or may be present in its subtle form even while we retain our focal object, just as prayer beads may be held quite slackly until one's grip becomes so loose that they fall from the hand. Kamalashila in *Stages of Meditation*[32] describes the coarsest form of slackness as resembling the darkness enveloping you if you if you are blind or have closed your eyes. Subtle slackness is present when intense clarity of the focal object diminishes. In this case, since slackness occurs in combination with meditative stabilization, it is virtuous. The coarser forms of slackness are unspecified as either virtuous or non-virtuous.

Sleep and lethargy are causes of slackness. Lethargy, which is an obstruction to liberation and never virtuous, is an aspect of confusion that makes the body and mind unserviceable and encourages the arising of disturbing emotions. It is an unspecified mental state in the upper realms and non-virtuous in the desire realm.

Not applying counteractions to slackness and excitement is the fourth fault which prevents achievement of a calmly abiding mind. This is avoided by responding promptly to the information provided by mental alertness and applying the appropriate remedies. The mental factor of intention, whose function is to move the mind towards a positive, negative or neutral object, plays a major role in this.

When subtle slackness arises the clarity of the object and the force of concentration diminish. It may be sufficient to intensify the attention and make the object appear more clearly. If this is ineffective, let go of the focal object and try to brighten up the mind. Slackness is a sign that the mind is too withdrawn and introverted.

To arouse joy and gain inspiration think about the teachings, especially about the feasibility of liberation and about the true paths of insight through which liberation is attained. Think about the enlightened ones, contemplating their complete elimination of faults and supreme development of good qualities, or about the spiritual community consisting of exalted beings, particularly Bodhisattvas on the Bodhisattva stages. The mind may also be enlivened by remembering that generosity unties the knot of miserliness and that giving our bodies, possessions and positive energy brings great benefits, or by thinking how ethical discipline, which forms the basis for all higher insights, especially for concentration and wisdom, leads to rebirth as a celestial being of the desire, form or formless realms and ultimately to the state of complete enlightenment.[33] Recalling the preciousness of this human life can also have a revitalizing effect. Then begin concentrating on the focal object once more.

If the slackness persists, stop the session and try to refresh yourself by splashing your face with water, sitting in a cool place where there is a breeze, taking a walk or looking at a panoramic view. When you feel invigorated begin a new session, but learn to be skillful in using your energy because forcing yourself to continue meditating at all costs is meaningless.

Subtle excitement occurs before distraction is fully present and feels as though one is just about to remember something. It arises when the mind is too tightly focused on the object. The initial remedy is to slacken the attention slightly. If this is not effective, let go of the focal object and think about impermanence and the imminence of death or about suffering, the defects of cyclic existence and the way in which disturbing emotions and contaminated actions control us. Any topic which is sobering and stops preoccupation with sense stimuli is appropriate. If the excitement persists, end the session. It may be helpful to cook a delicious meal, as eating somewhat rich and nutritious food decreases tension, settles the energy winds and makes one feel more relaxed.

When slackness or excitement are pronounced, it is customary to let go of the focal object and think about something else. Resuming concentration on the focal object after this is called cultivating fresh mindfulness. When the slackness or excitement are subtle, adjustments are made to the intensity of concentration and so forth while attention on the focal object is maintained. This is called cultivating old mindfulness.

A story is told about a competition between a skilled swordsman and an archer. No matter how many arrows the archer shot, the swordsman's whirling sword deflected and cut them down. When the archer had only one arrow left and was afraid that he would lose the competition, his wife, who was very beautiful, had an idea. She said, "I'll take a stroll across the field. The moment he catches sight of me, shoot your last arrow." She walked out, the swordsman saw her, was distracted by desire and the archer's arrow mortally wounded him. As he lay dying he said, "Not the arrow but my own lack of mindfulness killed me."

Between sessions it is important to counteract the causes of slackness and excitement by controlling your senses. This doesn't mean that you should not look, listen, smell, taste or touch, but when you have the choice, avoid what is unwholesome and prevent disturbing emotions from arising in response to sense stimuli. This demands continual mindfulness and vigilance.

It is wise to eat moderately. A nagging stomach because of too little food will spoil your concentration. If you eat till you need to loosen your belt, you will be much too full and sleepy to meditate. Since sleeping too much leads to the habit of dozing whenever there is an opportunity, and over-indulgence in sensual pleasures makes you lethargic, it is important to find the right balance.

When all is going well in the meditation, it is a fault to apply counteractions and you should leave well alone. This is called giving up effort, but only effort in the application of counteractions. Intensity of attention must still be maintained. The problem of applying unnecessary remedies does not arise until the ninth stage of developing a calmly abiding mind has been attained. By this stage single-pointed concentration can be maintained for as long as one wishes the session to last, but a calmly abiding mind has not yet been attained.

The bliss of perfect mental and physical pliancy is prevented by physical and mental resistance to engaging in virtue. It is usually said that mental pliancy is attained first. When all resistance to mental engagement in virtue is overcome, the energy winds flowing through the body become serviceable. This gives rise to physical pliancy and the resulting physical bliss induces mental bliss. Intense joy is experienced and when this stabilizes, calm abiding has been attained. The initial joy is compared to the jittery feeling you get when you receive some very good news. With the attainment of calm abiding a mental state of the upper realms and one which is the outcome of meditation is experienced for the first time.

People often want concise instructions on how to attain calm abiding and do not see the need to refer to the great texts. But if you are about to take a journey to a distant place, you must either know the way from your own previous experience or must rely on a good friend or on accurate instructions to guide you. If you just wander off on your own, you are unlikely to reach your destination. You must be equipped with full knowledge of how to practice, otherwise you will not recognize obstacles, know how to remove them or how to enhance the meditative stabilization gained. Your spiritual teacher's guidance is essential for this and if you intend to practice in solitude, your teacher should always be included within the boundary you set around your meditation place.

In his *Summary of the Stages of the Path* Tsongkhapa says:

> Concentration is a king with dominion over the mind,
> Once placed, immovable like the king of mountains.
> When directed it engages with every kind of virtuous object
> And induces the great bliss of a malleable body and mind.
> Knowing this, powerful yogis continually practice
> Meditative stabilization which defeats
> All inimical distraction.

Chapter Six
Wisdom

When one has gained a calmly abiding mind, the seven preparatory stages[34] and the concentrations of the form and formless realms can be developed. The prime purpose for developing a calmly abiding mind is as a basis for special insight. Those of the highest calibre use this powerful tool for the analysis of the four noble truths and to investigate reality in order to rid themselves of the disturbing emotions and free themselves from cyclic existence. When such highly developed concentration is accompanied not just by lack of attachment to this life but by a lack of attachment to future lives within cyclic existence, it becomes an authentic spiritual path, since the wish for freedom is present. When it is accompanied by the altruistic intention, it becomes a Bodhisattva practice.

Once you have a calmly abiding mind, you can sustain concentration even during ordinary activities. The bliss of pliancy reinforces calm abiding and vice versa, just as a comfortable bed helps you to sleep well and when you sleep well the bed feels comfortable.

Nagarjuna in his *Hundred Verses on Wisdom*[35] says:

> The root of all visible and invisible
> Good qualities is wisdom.
> Thus to accomplish both of these
> Hold firmly onto wisdom.

Knowledge or wisdom is the root of all the good qualities we can develop in this and future lives. It is therefore worth making effort to gain it, for without it our meditation is based on blind faith. Yet knowledge which lacks a firm foundation of genuine faith can be dangerous, since one may be tempted to use it unethically. To develop both faith and knowledge study the sutras and great texts, hear and think about the teachings, discuss them to clarify doubts, keep the company of intelligent friends and make offerings of light to create favorable causes for mental illumination.

It is said that in one of his previous lives the Buddha's disciple Shariputra, renowned for his profound understanding of reality, was a tailor who set up a light while he was sewing at night. He placed it in front of the image of an enlightened being and this had far-reaching consequences. It is also told that one of the causes for his great wisdom was a gift of needles and thread that he had made in a past life to a monk who sewed for the ordained community.

Once we appreciate the benefits that knowing reality brings, we will take a greater interest in it. The Buddha said that just as a few drops of healing nectar cures all sickness, the clear-light nectar of emptiness removes all the internal and external troubles of those who discover it.

Since most people's minds are not sufficiently developed and receptive, there is a danger that they will misunderstand what is taught. To ordinary appearances, therefore, the Buddha did not teach for some time after his enlightenment, but is said to have remained in the forest in silence. Then Brahma and Indra reminded him that he had originally vowed to attain enlightenment for the sake of all living beings and had for their sake amassed merit and insight for a very long period of time. They offered the Buddha a thousand-spoked golden wheel, requesting him to teach.[36] The Buddha inspired Brahma and Indra to do this in order to demonstrate the preciousness of the teachings and to let it be known that one should not teach without having been requested. It is also important always to ascertain whether the desired teaching is appropriate for the person who has requested it, since the purpose of the teachings is to bring benefit.

A complete understanding of reality frees us from cyclic existence, but even a partial understanding leads to happiness in good rebirths. It is therefore wise to investigate the nature of reality, particularly the nature of the self. In *Yogic Deeds of Bodhisattvas* Aryadeva says:

> Correct perception [leads to] the supreme state,
> Some perception to good rebirths.
> The wise thus always expand their intelligence
> To think about the inner nature.

If understanding reality has such profound implications, why don't more people understand it? Since our intelligence and enthusiasm are limited, we find reality hard to understand, and though its understanding brings such inconceivable benefits, those who have gained it are as rare as stars in the daytime. Nevertheless, take courage, for if you have enough enthusiasm, you, too, can discover this precious nectar.

Interest in reality means not merely idle curiosity but a real determination to discover how things actually exist. Aryadeva also says:

> Those with little merit
> Do not even doubt this teaching.
> Entertaining just a doubt
> Tears to tatters worldly existence.

Many people don't even begin to wonder about the nature of reality, which is that all things lack inherent existence and at the same time function in a perfectly satisfactory way. Even a positive doubt regarding this tears the fabric of cyclic existence apart. Why? Because for the brief moment during which we wonder whether it is true, we take reality to mind. That small effort may eventually lead us to establish the nature of reality for ourselves through scriptural passages and reasoning.

In his commentary on Aryadeva's *Yogic Deeds of Bodhisattvas* Chandrakirti tells the story of a ship's captain who is captured by an ogress. She warns him never even to look, let alone venture, to the south of her island. This admonition arouses his curiosity. One day he evades her watchful eyes and steals away to explore. There, in the south, he finds the king of horses, Balahaka, who will carry you away across the ocean to safety on the other shore if you hold on to even one hair of his mane. And so the ship's captain escaped from the island on which he had been held prisoner.

In just such a way, investigating reality and holding on to even a single line of reasoning that establishes emptiness will free you from the prison of desire, hostility and confusion.

The *Treatise on the Middle Way*[37] is the root or foundation for all Nagarjuna's other works which deal with Madhyamika philosophy. The view of the middle way propounded in them is the basis of sutra and tantra and is the highest philosophical system in the Buddhist traditions of India and Tibet. There is no clearer nor more subtle view of reality and I doubt that there ever will be one.

In his *Praise of Dependent Arising*,[38] in which he expresses his gratitude to the Buddha for explaining the dependently arising nature of things, Tsongkhapa says:

> The many troubles of the world
> Have their root in ignorance.
> [The Buddha] taught dependent arising,
> Through seeing which ignorance stops.

The world here refers to our contaminated aggregates. They and the person attributed to them undergo constant change and disintegration. One who takes on these contaminated aggregates over and over again and cannot get rid of them is a worldly person, a person in cyclic existence. In fact, although we speak of the body and mind as though we own them, it is impossible clearly to separate self from body and mind.

The troubles to which Tsongkhapa refers are birth, ageing, sickness and death, being separated from what we like, not getting what we want and getting what we do not want. These troubles affect us all, but in addition we each experience our share of personal physical and mental difficulties. We are so accustomed to all this that we no longer notice just how painful it is, except when the suffering becomes intense.

All these troubles stem from contaminated actions and disturbing emotions. The imprints of past contaminated actions are activated by desire and new contaminated actions are initiated by ignorance. This ignorance is the notion that the person and other phenomena have inherent existence, and it can only be uprooted by an understanding diametrically opposed to it, namely that the person and other phenomena are empty of any inherent existence. The Buddha's teaching of dependent arising leads to this understanding, which bears different results depending upon the attitudes which accompany it, the length of time taken to cultivate it and the intelligence of the practitioner.

The eighteenth chapter of Nagarjuna's *Treatise on the Middle Way* explains how to meditate on the selflessness of persons and other phenomena. For whom is it intended? Though other beings may be able to make use of it, it is most certainly intended for us humans with an interest in reality. But Nagarjuna's great work cannot bring about any change in us if we do not take an active part. Can we say Nagarjuna's teaching is alive if it remains between the covers of a book or is neatly wrapped in brocade and placed on a shelf like a museum piece?

Intelligence, interest and effort are needed to understand reality, but faith is also mentioned as a prerequisite. The kind of faith which appreciates the benefits of gaining an understanding of reality gives rise to aspiration and effort. However, the faith which is the principal basis and prerequisite for the development of wisdom is conviction regarding the connection between actions and their effects.

In the *Precious Garland* Nagarjuna says:

> High status is considered to be happiness,
> Definite goodness to be liberation.
> In summary the means to accomplish them
> Are briefly faith and wisdom.

These words sum up the essence of the practices which yield a good rebirth as well as liberation and enlightenment. Of the two, faith and wisdom, the latter is the more important, since it alone can free us completely from cyclic existence. Yet conviction regarding the connection between actions and their effects is essential if we hope to attain the good rebirths we will need until we gain liberation. Understanding reality strengthens our belief in the relationship between actions and their effects.

Does investigating the nature of our mind bring the same results as investigating the nature of reality? We can speak about the conventional nature and the ultimate nature of the mind. The conventional aspect is primarily its luminous and cognizant nature, which is unique to consciousness and is not shared by other phenomena. Its ultimate nature is the same as that of all other phenomena. Only the bases of emptiness differ but emptiness itself is always the same. Once one has understood the emptiness of a single phenomenon, it is easy to understand the emptiness of others. By overcoming the misconception which holds things to have inherent existence, we will rid ourselves of the disturbing attitudes and emotions which imprison us in cyclic existence.

A misinterpretation of certain sutra passages, which state that everything is mere conceptuality, merely imputed and in the nature of mind, is the mistaken notion that everything is mind. Since the mind is unfindable as something with shape or color, one might then conclude that it has no existence and that, therefore, nothing else exists either. Focusing on this absence, one might wrongly assume that one had gained an understanding of emptiness.

If your approach to reality is to have some real meaning in terms of your experience and not remain at the level of intellectual speculation, you must follow the Buddha's presentation of the four noble truths, first contemplating the suffering you and others share. Once you feel a genuine sense of aversion to it, search for its causes. When you recognize these to be your own contaminated actions and emotions which spring from ignorance, you understand that whether or not you gain freedom from your present condition depends on whether or not you can get rid of this ignorance. That is the key.

Not every thought "I" is a misconception of the self. The misconception is one which takes the self to exist objectively, from its own side, as it appears. This innate conception of "I" and "mine" clings to the self and demands its happiness. Everything considered as "mine" appears intended to insure this. Disturbing emotions arise as a result and instigate actions which lead to suffering. The false view of the transitory collection[39] as a real "I" and "mine" underlies all our miseries.

The only way to overcome it is to disprove the existence of what it clings to—an objectively existent self. This is the object of negation. When this fabricated self is seen to have no existence, the false view will stop. What remains when the existence of the self as it appears has been disproved is the self as it actually exists. Only the fabrication, the self as it appears to exist, is refuted.

The object of negation by reasoning is something totally non-existent, otherwise how could its non-existence be established by logic? On the other hand, our misconception of the self is at present very much existent, but by understanding the non-existence of the object to which it clings, it will gradually cease. Thus the object of negation by the path is something which exists but which is eliminated through practice.

When beginning the search for the self as it appears, you must first identify exactly what is being sought. Just faith in the statements of your teachers and of the great masters that nothing has true existence cannot bring about a shift in your perceptions. Repeating it to yourself when you sit down to meditate can implant valuable imprints, but cannot induce the conviction of personal experience.

Having recognized the importance of negating true existence and understanding that it is done through reasoning, one might conclude that this is to be accomplished while studying the teachings and thinking about them, but that during meditation one's mind should be free from all conceptuality. This is a mistake. In his *Supplement to the Middle Way* the great master Chandrakirti says:

> When the mind sees that all disturbing emotions and faults
> Arise from the view of the transitory collection,
> And understanding that the self is its object,
> The yogi refutes the self.

A yogi is one who practices meditation. Understanding that the false view of the transitory collection takes as its object the actual self and distorts it, the meditator refutes the truly existent self.

If one is incapable of establishing the nature of reality through reasoning, but has faith in one's spiritual teacher's assertion that everything is selfless and keeps this in mind, though it is not meditation on emptiness, it has the power to purify many karmic obstructions and creates valuable imprints for a future understanding. In sutra there are statements that faith and belief in emptiness can even purify the gravest actions such as killing one's parents. Still, since we claim to be intelligent, we should not be content with mere faith, but should follow the methods for understanding reality laid out by the exalted father Nagarjuna and his spiritual sons, Aryadeva and Chandrakirti. Just mentioning their names gives me happiness.

They established the nature of reality through many different avenues of reasoning, but one which is relatively easy to understand is the reason of not being one or many. In this approach there are four essential points. The first is to identify clearly the object of refutation, namely what is sought. This is the self as it appears to the instinctive sense of "I." Then we must gain certainty that if the self existed as it appears, there could only be two possibilities: either it should be totally identical with the aggregates that constitute body and mind or distinct from them.[40]

The search is then made until it is evident that the self cannot be found as inseparably one with the aggregates or as distinct from them. If you have lost a cow and intend to search for it, you would make sure you know what the cow looks like. Is it a dun cow or a black and white cow? Does it have long or short horns? Then you must know where to look and feel certain that if it isn't in those places, it has really gone. You search the first field looking in every corner and behind every bush, but you can't find it. Then you begin searching the other field, behind the boulders down by the river, in the copse of trees, everywhere, but it is not there either. At this point you are vividly aware of the cow's absence.

Meditating on emptiness is not just a matter of sitting down and beginning. Any authentic Buddhist practice is preceded by taking sincere refuge. This entails certain prerequisite attitudes, understanding what we take refuge in, how to take refuge and the commitments involved.[41] It is impossible to take real refuge unless you feel aversion to cyclic existence and trust the Three Jewels. But you also cannot take refuge unless you know about the enlightened ones, their teaching and the spiritual community. When you take refuge, you entrust yourself to the enlightened ones, like a sick person who turns to a physician. You look upon the teachings as your medicine and the spiritual community as your care-givers. Your aim is to achieve good health and a cure from the sickness which afflicts you. Understanding what it means to take refuge and actually taking refuge will only be effective if you keep the commitments.

Next you think about living beings and how they have all been your mothers, fathers, brothers and sisters in countless past lives, how they have nurtured and shown you kindness, and how through their misconception of the self they are bound in cyclic existence, experiencing many kinds of physical and mental suffering, including birth, sickness, ageing and death. This is not a fairy-tale. Just look around! Evidence of their suffering confronts you everywhere. Try to feel a close connection to them, to see them as near and dear and then think of their suffering and of how they lack even ordinary happiness, let alone lasting transcendent happiness.

The more lovable they appear, the more their suffering will move you, arousing the wish to free them from it and give them happiness. If you don't feel real affection for them, you may well feel satisfied to see those you dislike suffer. Don't be dismayed by the fact that you don't find all living creatures lovable at present. Learning to see them in this way takes concerted effort and much analytical meditation.

It is easier to recognize their suffering than to see them as lovable, but even then we tend only to feel compassionate towards those who are destitute or obviously in need and not towards those who wear designer labels and drive smart cars. Yet all ordinary living beings have that basic misconception of the self from which the disturbing emotions arise and all suffer in a multitude of ways.

Though you feel determined to alleviate their suffering and give them happiness, the enormity of this task in view of your own present limited abilities seems overwhelming. You therefore resolve to attain enlightenment exclusively for their sake and for this reason you undertake to meditate on emptiness. Your meditation on emptiness becomes a practice of the Great Vehicle if these are the thoughts and feelings that motivate it. Taking sincere refuge and generating the altruistic intention qualitatively changes the practices of hearing, thinking and meditating.

This should be followed by a short or long session of devotion to the spiritual teacher. Visualize your spiritual teacher in the form of the Buddha, as your meditational deity or in his or her own form and then perform the seven-part practice to purify negativities and create positive energy.[42] Make a long or short mandala offering and request blessings that your mind may turn towards the teachings, that you may practice them without obstacles, and that you may overcome distorted ways of thinking, cultivate undistorted ones and develop love, compassion, the altruistic intention and understanding of reality through which to rid yourself of the confusion at the root of cyclic existence. This opens your heart to the warmth of blessings and prepares your mind for meditation.

Now, sitting in a good meditation posture,[43] begin with the first of the four points of analysis. Create the intention to recognize how the self appears to the instinctive thought "I." Then relax and try to rest the mind in a natural and uncontrived state for some time without allowing it to drift into distraction. The thought "I" may come up of its own accord. If it doesn't, invite it. How does the self appear to this thought "I"?

When trying to identify the self for which a search is to be made and whose existence will be negated, the guidance of our teachers and of past masters, who have gained personal experience in this, is essential because they tell us that if the "I" appears in this or that way, we still have not actually identified the object of refutation correctly.

Both the normal thought "I" and conceptions of the self focus on the validly existing self. We know the self exists, for we can validly make statements like "I am sitting," "I am eating," "I am comfortable," "I am happy." If there were no self at all such statements would be meaningless. But how does this self actually exist? It exists nominally, as attributed by name and thought to the aggregates and not from its own side as it appears to exist.

Mere attribution by name and thought is the subtle level of conventional existence. If one fails to establish this level of existence, one will also fail to establish the fundamental nature of things correctly. When the two truths, the conventional and ultimate, cannot be established, there is no possibility of liberation. Liberation depends on understanding emptiness, but a correct and undistorted understanding of the conventional is the indispensable basis for approaching the ultimate or fundamental nature of reality. Emptiness cannot be understood unless one knows what is empty of inherent existence and the reasons which establish emptiness, such as the reason of dependent arising. These are conventional phenomena.

How does the "I" appear? As discrete and not associated with body and mind, as existing under its own power, in and of itself. This is the appearance of true existence, yet nothing exists in this way. Nothing exists as it appears. Until we know what we are looking for, we cannot understand its absence. Once the object of negation has been identified correctly, emptiness is relatively easy to understand.

Imagine you are groping in the dark for a pot. When your hands touch it, you think, "That's it," and the pot doesn't seem at all like something designated by thought. It seems very real and hard and quite objectively existent from its own side. Recognizing the object of refutation is difficult. Everything that appears to our mind and senses seems to exist objectively and not as designated by thought. This is how things appear to ordinary beings and why it is said that all their perceptions, even valid perceptions, are mistaken. Since the conventional valid perceptions of sentient beings are affected by the imprints of ignorance, they are mistaken from the point of view that everything appears truly existent to them.

When we assent to this appearance with regard to the self, we hold a conception of a self of persons and when we assent to it in the case of other things, such as the body or mind, we hold a conception of a self of phenomena. These misconceptions are the root of cyclic existence and the way to overcome them is to understand that the object to which they adhere does not exist at all. Only then will these innate conceptions cease.

Meditation on selflessness is not done by withdrawing the mind from conceptions of a self, in the way that one stops thinking about something which has been bothering one. Meditation on selflessness involves identifying the object of negation, the seemingly inherently existent self, and then coming to understand the absence of such a self.

———————◆———————

The eighteenth chapter of Nagarjuna's *Treatise on the Middle Way* consists of twelve verses which summarize the contents of the earlier and later parts of the book and present them in terms of practice. In the *Ocean of Reasoning*,[44] his commentary on Nagarjuna's text, Tsongkhapa devotes extensive attention to identifying the object of negation, emphasizing the fact that everything is imputed by thought with the corollary that nothing exists which is not so.

Throughout his *Great Exposition of the Stages of the Path*, from the section dealing with cultivation of the relationship with the spiritual teacher, in which his or her qualities and kindness are emphasized, to the part concerned with the attainment of Buddhahood, Tsongkhapa seeks to make us aware of things as they actually are. The great texts repeatedly stress the need to establish impermanence and selflessness, but where are they to be established? Not in things, since impermanence and selflessness are a natural part of them anyway, but in our minds.

All products of causes and conditions are totally unstable and change moment by moment. When we reflect on this, we know it to be true, yet such things appear lasting and unchanging. Our problems stem from the fact that we assent to this appearance and act on it. Everything that exists does so in relation to and depending upon other factors, yet things seem to exist independently and objectively. This mode of existence is the object of refutation. The aim of meditation on impermanence and selflessness is to enable us to see things as they actually are. In both cases they seem to exist one way but actually exist in another.

If the self existed the way it appears, it should be findable and there are only two possibilities: either it is one with body and mind or it is distinct from them. The impossibility of the latter mode of existence is relatively easy to establish, for if the self were distinct, it should still be demonstrable when every element of body and mind is eliminated. Normally we don't think about this at all, but when we do, we can see that the self could not possibly exist in this way.

We then search to locate the self within the body and mind. In the *Precious Garland* Nagarjuna demonstrates how the self is not any of the body parts which he refers to in terms of six constituent elements. The self is not any of the hard parts of the body, like the teeth, nails, skin or bones, which constitute the earth element. Nor is it the water element, all the body fluids such as urine, spittle, sweat, tears or blood. Nor is it the body heat, the fire element, the breath which is the wind element or the orifices which are the space element. None of these body parts reveals a self. When we begin to search the mind, we find the self is not any of the different forms of consciousness either.

The validly existing self cannot be found either when we search for it, but in that case unfindability does not imply non-existence but simply deceptive existence. Here, however, we are searching for the self as an objectively existent entity, which is how it appears to exist. Anything objectively existent should be findable and in this case unfindability denotes the non-existence of what is sought.

In the *Precious Garland* Nagarjuna points out that also the sum of all these parts that make up the six constituents—earth, water, fire, air, space and consciousness—is not the self. The whole forms the basis of designation for the self. The basis of designation is not that which is designated to it and vice versa. The self is like that which takes on the aggregates, the aggregates that which is taken on. Not finding the self which is sought signifies that the self has no objective existence but is a mere imputation dependent on other factors. The same search can also be made for individual body parts, such as the hand.

There definitely is a self. It seems to exist from the side of the aggregates, and as long as we are content to leave it at that, everything functions satisfactorily, but when we begin to search for the self, it cannot be found. Thus the self is false and deceptive, since it appears in one way and exists in another. It is a mere appearance, merely imputed, a mere name, but does not exist as it appears. To gain a real understanding of Nagarjuna's approach, we must consider it repeatedly and try to recognize what he is describing within our own experience.

The Perfection of Wisdom sutras explicitly teach the nature of reality, emptiness of inherent existence. The hidden content of these sutras is the explanation of the stages of the path. Nagarjuna is the greatest commentator on these sutras to have emerged and we cannot do better than to follow his elucidation of their subject-matter. By studying and thinking about what the Buddha and Nagarjuna taught we keep the teachings alive. Great masters through the ages have stressed the importance of the living tradition and have sought to pass on the teachings to us as if they were live coals. When the coals grow cold we throw them out. No real benefit, namely a transformation in our way of thinking and feeling, can occur without this living tradition in which the teachings are passed down from teacher to student.

These days the special relationship that existed in the past between students and teachers has become unfashionable, but once students quite naturally took off their shoes when they approached their teacher's door and spoke softly out of respect. This was voluntary, not enforced, and did not need to be taught, since it belonged to a way of life that they could observe around them. Complete trust, mutual respect and a sense of commitment are the essential basis for a successful relationship between teacher and student.

All the things we perceive appear to be intrinsically existent. They exist but not as they appear. Our tendency to treat things as though they were unchanging and independently existent brings us pain. Friends and enemies seem fixed in their roles and power, authority and wealth seem lasting. The teachings contradict these appearances, not to add to our unhappiness, but to help us recognize our true situation so that we can find happiness.

Surely the self must be distinct from the aggregates, otherwise what goes on to other lives? The self and the aggregates are different but they are one entity. For example, the self is not a separate entity from the hand, otherwise we couldn't say, "He touched me" when someone touches our hand, or "I'm in pain" when we have hurt our hand. The self of the past and the self of the future are all parts of the continuum of the self, but the self of this life ceases at death.

The self that is sitting down and the self that is standing belong to one continuum but are not one entity. My hand when I was sitting down is not one entity with my self when I have stood up. My hand as it was when I was sitting down no longer exists by the time I am standing. The coarse aggregates of this life cease at death and there is no further continuum of a similar type, whereas although the self of this life also ceases at death, there is a further continuum of a similar type.

Dying is the process which precedes death. Actual death and the beginning of the intermediate state are simultaneous. While the coarse energy winds and states of consciousness are active, the subtle ones are not, but as soon as the coarse ones cease to operate, the subtle ones begin. In the intermediate state we also have a body, but like a dream body it is much more subtle than our present body. In that state our subtle energy wind and subtle mental consciousness act as the basis of imputation for the continuing "I."

Sutra does not discuss the subtle energy winds and consciousness because the main purpose of the Buddha's teaching in the sutras is to help us avoid coarser unwholesome physical and verbal activities. These are stopped through the practice of ethical discipline. Only then can we eliminate the more subtle impediments to the perfection of concentration, which acts as a basis for the development of wisdom. Without purifying the coarser mental stains first, we cannot hope to remove the subtle ones. In sutra only conceptions of true existence are mentioned as the root of cyclic existence, but tantra cites both these conceptions and the energy winds they ride.

The Tibetan master Jangkya Rolpay Dorjay[45] wrote a short work called *Recognizing the Mother* about understanding reality. In many texts reality and the understanding of reality are referred to as the mother. A mother is one who has given birth. The children of this mother are the four kinds of exalted ones who have passed beyond the paths of ordinary beings: exalted Hearers, exalted Solitary Realizers, exalted Bodhisattvas and exalted Buddhas.

Jangkya Rolpay Dorjay speaks of how the mother is present all the time but the small crazy child has lost and cannot find her. This means that the mind's fundamental nature is always present with the mind, but we are unaware of this. The mind searching for reality is referred to as a small crazy child. By fortunate circumstance big brother dependent arising whispers the secret which leads to discovery—the reason of dependent arising leads to discovery of the nature of reality. Whispering refers to the fact that at first the nature of reality is understood inferentially and only later directly.

Then the child exclaims, "It is, it is! No, no, it's not!" When no examination is made, things seem to exist from their own side, but as soon as one starts searching nothing can be found.

Mother, the understanding of reality, and father, skillful means, must be inseparably unified. Fostering qualities of purity in the form of ethically sound conduct, qualities of kindness by helping and not harming others, and qualities of understanding, through which we know what to do, leads to complete development. The disturbing emotions, which spring from our clinging to a self that does not exist, obstruct our peace and happiness. This clinging can only be overcome by understanding that its object is totally non-existent.

The body and mind and the self are different, but the self cannot be isolated from the body and mind. The self and the aggregates are one entity and exist in mutual dependence. This is their conventional mode of existence. However, the self appears not to need to depend on anything. As has already been explained, if it existed as it appears, it would be inherently existent and should be findable.

Holding on to the object of refutation, you must gain certainty that if the self existed as it appears, it could only be inseparably one and identical with body and mind or quite distinct from them and that there is no third possibility. Easier said than done! Anyone who is really determined to meditate on the nature of the self must spend plenty of time observing how it appears in different situations. The self for which you will search should seem palpably clear.

Now let us follow some of Nagarjuna's arguments. If the self were one with the aggregates, there couldn't be an owner of the aggregates and that which is owned. Valid conventional cognition posits the two as different. This is not invalidated by any other valid conventional cognition nor by the reasoning cognition which investigates the ultimate.[46] Moreover, if the self and the aggregates were one, there should either be five selves since there are five aggregates or only one aggregate since there is one self.

At the end of this life when the body is cremated the self would necessarily discontinue. In that case, how would memory of past lives by ordinary people without clairvoyant powers be possible?

If the self and the aggregates were inherently distinct, namely totally unrelated, the characteristics of the aggregates—production, duration and disintegration—would not pertain to the self. The self would then be a non-product.

Characteristics of the body such as dimension would not apply to the self and one couldn't say, "I'm tall." Feelings would be unrelated to the self and one couldn't say, "I'm happy." Recognitions like "This is a dog" would be unrelated to the self and one couldn't say, "I've seen the dog." Furthermore when the aggregates are eliminated, a discretely existent self should be findable.

In his *Supplement to the Middle Way* Chandrakirti says:

> The mind itself creates the world of living beings
> And the extremely diverse world which is the container.
> It is said that beings without exception arise from actions.
> If the mind is eliminated, there are also no actions.

Both the physical world, referred to as the container, and its contents, the living beings, are created by mind. The Buddha said that we ourselves and our environment are the result of past actions. The bodies and minds of living beings result from their previous personal actions, while the environment, which we share with others, comes into being through communally performed actions. These may be virtuous or non-virtuous. Virtuous actions result in happiness and a wholesome environment. A mixture of virtuous and non-virtuous actions leads to mixed results and wholly non-virtuous actions lead to suffering and an insalubrious environment. Activities of body and speech come from intention which is present because there is mental activity.

Since happiness and unhappiness depend on whether the mind is in a peaceful or unpeaceful condition, training the mind is our principal task. We are personally responsible for our happiness. Virtuous actions create personal and common good, while disturbing emotions make the mind unpeaceful and give rise to actions which upset others and destroy their peace.

When the mind is dominated by disturbing emotions it becomes turbid and we cannot see clearly. Like water, the mind is pure by nature and the pollutant factors are extraneous. Just as a crystal is used to purify water and remove pollutants, the mind is purified of these emotions by applying antidotes to them. Since the mind can be freed from all faults and can develop marvelous qualities, its basic nature and thus the nature of living beings is pure and good.

It is said that all living beings have Buddha-nature because they possess this basic purity and everything necessary for inner development. The fundamental nature and purity of an ordinary being's mind is no different from that of a Buddha. Since mental stains are temporary, we are not condemned to stay the way we are but can attain enlightenment, provided we have enough energy and enthusiasm.

The cause of our present condition is ignorance regarding reality. Not only do we not know how things actually exist, but we distort their mode of existence. By understanding reality correctly we can rid ourselves of the three poisons, of actions based on them and of the consequent suffering. It is therefore of paramount importance to understand, control and transform our various mental activities. The impetus to do this comes not from some imposed discipline but arises naturally from understanding the value of mental control.

When you analyze to discover whether the self, which seems to exist objectively, is inseparably one with the aggregates or distinct from them, it cannot be found. Though this unfindability denotes that the self has no inherent existence, at that time during the meditation you do not think, "This means the self isn't inherently existent," nor "The self has no inherent existence, but there is a nominally existent self." A mere non-affirming negation or mere absence appears to the mind.

Experiencing the absence of what you were looking for is a glimpse of the right view. Attention is sustained on this until it starts to fade. You then induce it again by means of analysis. Although you are unable to enter into proper meditative equipoise at present, you approximate the "space-like meditative equipoise"[47] focusing on the absence or emptiness of what was sought.

When you arise from this meditation, the "I" once more appears and the thought "I" again arises. Now, through the force of the preceding meditation, you understand that the "I" appears but is empty and though empty it appears. It is therefore false like a magical illusion.[48] Anyone who is accustomed to mirrors knows that the reflection of their face is not a real face, yet they still perceive the face that appears in the mirror.

The thought "I" and "mine" are constantly present. You may think you don't see the "I" and "mine" as inherently existent, but as soon as anyone makes the slightest accusation or criticism or when any provocation occurs, the "I" and "mine" loom large, seem very real and not at all merely attributed to body and mind.

The *Treatise on the Middle Way* says that having established the non-inherent existence of the "I," how could the "mine" have any inherent existence? The *King of Meditative Stabilizations Sutra* advises that we should first establish the lack of inherent existence of the person, namely of "I" and "mine," and then that of other phenomena. While there is no difference in subtlety between the selflessness of the person and that of other phenomena, there are many differences between the bases of selflessness. It is therefore said to be somewhat easier to understand the selflessness of the person compared to that of other phenomena, because it is impossible to think of the person except in reference to the body and mind. One cannot take someone to mind without thinking of their aggregates, the basis of designation for that person. This clearly indicates the dependently arising nature of the person.

The awareness which apprehends the unfindability and thus the non-inherent existence of the "I" does not apprehend the non-inherent existence of the "mine," but by the force of the reasoning which establishes the non-inherent existence of the "I," the non-inherent existence of the "mine" will be understood through a mere shift of attention. Once we have understood the emptiness of the "I" and "mine," we have found the view which is diametrically opposed to the misconceptions which form the root of cyclic existence. By familiarizing ourselves with this we will eventually eliminate the disturbing emotions and attain liberation.

When the false view of the transitory collection is dispelled by the correct understanding of how the "I" and "mine" exist, we continue to accustom ourselves to it until the subjective apprehending awareness and emptiness, the apprehended object, are experienced as one and no conventionalities of any kind appear to the mind. This experience denotes a high level of realization. When emptiness is first understood, it is cognized by way of a mental image which prevents clarity. At that time conventionalities are still strongly apparent, but as the practice is continued through the paths of accumulation and preparation, which precede direct cognition of emptiness, the veils imposed by the mental image grow thinner and emptiness becomes clearer. On the last moment of the path of preparation the veils fall away and all signs of conventional existence are pacified. The path of seeing is attained when emptiness is perceived directly.

Conceptions of inherent existence can be overcome through this understanding because it is a way of apprehending reality completely antithetical to the way in which the conception of inherent existence apprehends it. Once emptiness has been established, it is necessary to develop a combination of calm abiding and special insight focusing on the non-inherent existence of the "I" and "mine." This is the way to banish forever all false views of the transitory collection.

Nagarjuna now answers an objection concerning the fact that there is a practitioner engaged in getting rid of the misconception of the "I" and "mine." Surely as long as such a practitioner exists, there must be a real "I" and "mine." When the non-inherent existence of the "I" and "mine" has already been conclusively established, what other kind of real "I" and "mine" could there be? As long as any clinging to an inherently existent "I" and "mine" persists, one has not understood emptiness. Without understanding emptiness the false view of the transitory collection cannot be dislodged and continues to act as a source for compulsive actions which keep one in cyclic existence.

By meditating on selflessness we overcome conceptions of a self, focusing on the inner "I" and on the outer "mine," as well as all the disturbing attitudes and emotions which spring from the false view of the transitory collection. In particular, here, Nagarjuna refers to four kinds of grasping. The first is grasping at the objects of desire, namely at sense stimuli. The second is grasping at views. These include wrong views, extreme views and views holding faulty discipline and conduct as supreme. The third is grasping at forms of discipline and conduct associated with bad views and the fourth is grasping at the false view of the transitory collection.[49] When these are overcome, actions projecting cyclic existence cease and birth within cyclic existence stops. This is the attainment of liberation.

Two perceptions of reality are at issue here. While the understanding of selflessness becomes clearer, the more reasoning and analysis one applies, conceptions of inherent existence cannot sustain logical scrutiny and are undermined by reasoning. Ignorance sets in motion fresh actions which continue cyclic existence. These actions cease in their second moment, leaving imprints which are later triggered by craving and grasping. When craving and grasping stop, even though imprints of past actions may still be present, they won't give rise to continued cyclic existence, just as a seed deprived of moisture will not sprout.

Cyclic existence is the state of being bound to the contaminated aggregates by the chains of compulsive action and disturbing emotions. Liberation is freedom from these chains. The person does not cease to exist when contaminated actions and disturbing emotions cease but experiences a state of freedom from suffering. When the different forms of craving and grasping stop, there is no clinging to this life nor grasping at a future life. Since their absence prevents the triggering of imprints, existence, the tenth link in the process, which is classed as action and marks the moment when the activated imprint is about to yield its outcome, does not occur. Without this there is no birth and consequently no sickness, ageing or death.[50]

Thus the ending of contaminated actions and disturbing emotions is liberation. But how are they ended? The actions spring from the disturbing emotions, in particular from attachment and aversion. Attachment and aversion arise when we encounter something attractive or unattractive and we respond with an incorrect mental approach which distorts and exaggerates the attractiveness or unattractiveness of the object. Attachment and aversion therefore arise from conceptuality.

This demonstrates that all the factors involved occur dependently and do not exist from their own side. The conceptuality of this incorrect mental approach comes from our clinging to what is said and the words saying it, to what is known and that which knows it, to what is produced and that which produces it, to men and women and to all things as truly existent. Throughout time without beginning we have been accustomed to seeing things this way. It can therefore be said that the incorrect mental approach arises from imprints. When we cut through the fabrications created by notions of true existence and understand these objects to be empty of inherent existence, the incorrect mental approach and all that derives from it stops.

In Aryadeva's *Yogic Deeds of Bodhisattvas*, which was written as a commentary on Nagarjuna's *Treatise on the Middle Way*, the eighth and twelfth chapters elucidate many points upon which Nagarjuna touches in his eighteenth chapter. Aryadeva says:

> In brief Tathagatas explain
> Virtue as non-violence
> And emptiness as nirvana—
> Here there are only these two.

The beginning of Nagarjuna's *Precious Garland* describes six-teen practices which lead to a high rebirth and liberation.[51] Nagarjuna indicates that any practice which does not consist of eliminating harm or accomplishing good is not an authentic practice of the Buddha's teaching. This is a criterion we might do well to consider. He says:

> Just mortifying the body is not
> Practice of the teachings because through this
> Harm to others is not eliminated
> Nor are others helped by it.

Emptiness is also referred to as "natural nirvana." Familiarizing ourselves with the understanding of emptiness, until subject and object become one taste and are like water poured into water, is the way to rid ourselves of the fabrications created by conceptuality and of their imprints. Such an understanding of emptiness is necessarily based upon meditative stabilization and this, in turn, requires a sound foundation of ethical discipline or non-violent conduct.

By listening to the teachings repeatedly, thinking about them and meditating in order to integrate them, they become thoroughly familiar. We begin to gain insights when our way of thinking accords with the teachings and we actually experience what is described. Our reluctance to think repeatedly and deeply about what we hear or read is a defensive mechanism because we do not really want to change. We would rather just listen to some new teachings or hear what is familiar expressed in an original or poetic way. Our deep-seated resistance prevents us from taking in what we hear or read and when we try to recall what was said, we can almost remember but not quite. In that case how can we expect our contact with the teachings to do anything more than leave some imprints?

The next objection which Nagarjuna answers regards the fact that since Buddhist texts repeatedly mention the importance of taming the self, there must be a self. Yet other passages say there is no self and there are no sentient beings. Why are there such contradictions?

These statements are not aimed at the same people. Some people deny that the self continues from one life to the next and that virtuous or non-virtuous actions in this life yield happiness or suffering in the future. People with such a lack of understanding are likely to perform many irresponsible and gravely negative actions. To them the Buddha said there is a real self to make them take care and to encourage them to perform positive actions which would protect them from bad rebirths. A skilled physician doesn't try to treat all of a patient's ailments simultaneously but treats first what requires immediate attention.

Others, who have already turned away from non-virtue and are actively engaged in virtue, nevertheless remain tightly bound to cyclic existence through conceptions of a self. Like a kite that can fly high but remains attached to a string, these people take good rebirths, even in the highest state of cyclic existence, called the "Peak of Existence," but cannot gain complete freedom because of their conceptions of a self. To loosen their hold on such conceptions the Buddha taught those with intermediate understanding coarser forms of selflessness.[52]

To those with the capacity to understand the profound and to those already familiar with teachings on reality, he taught that both the self and selflessness are empty of inherent existence. Thus his different statements were intended to lead gradually towards the deepest understanding.

The precious elixir of teaching on emptiness should not be poured into a vessel without first examining it. If the recipients are not sufficiently prepared for this teaching, they may interpret lack of inherent existence to mean total non-existence and fail to make a distinction between wholesome and unwholesome actions. They might then feel at liberty to perform seriously negative actions. Of course, from the point of view of their fundamental nature, wholesome and unwholesome actions are exactly the same, but conventionally there is a great difference. In *Yogic Deeds of Bodhisattvas* Aryadeva says:

> First prevent the demeritorious,
> Next prevent [ideas of a coarse] self.
> Later prevent views of all kinds.
> Whoever knows of this is wise.

Someone who first concentrates on teaching the connection between actions and their effects to prevent demeritorious activities, then explains the coarser forms of selflessness to overcome intellectually formed conceptions of a self and finally teaches that both the self and selflessness lack inherent existence to stop all wrong views is a skillful teacher. A skilled dietician may first prescribe a low-fat diet and later a much richer one when the patient's system is strong enough to digest it.

The teaching of emptiness is a very powerful medicine because through it we can completely destroy the root of cyclic existence. In the *Heart Sutra*[53] it is referred to as the mantra that totally pacifies all suffering. A mantra is something that protects the mind, yet like anti-venom it can prove dangerous when given to the wrong person.

For both Buddhists and non-Buddhists who believe there is a connection between actions and their effects, ascertaining the nature of the self is important. Some think of the self as permanent because they cannot accept that something which is produced and disintegrates moment by moment could be the agent of actions and experiencer of their results. Others, failing to establish a continuity for the self or living beings, conclude through seemingly correct reasoning that the self has no continuing existence and could not therefore in a future life experience the results of wholesome or unwholesome actions performed in this life. Failure to differentiate between lack of inherent existence and non-existence causes much confusion. Though the self is neither permanent nor independent, the conventionally existent self does come from past lives and continues into future ones.

If the Buddha taught that both the self and selflessness lack intrinsic existence, what did he say exists? Neither the subject-matter and the words expressing it, nor the mind and its field of activity have any ultimate existence, but they do exist conventionally. Verbal descriptions of reality can never evoke an exalted being's vivid and stark experience of reality, nor can conceptual thought apprehend it as exalted beings do. The praise to the perfection of wisdom, said to have been spoken by Rahula, the Buddha's son, in honor of his mother, refers to this:

> To the inconceivable, inexpressible perfection of wisdom,
> Whose space-like nature is unproduced and does not cease,
> The sphere of activity of the exalted wisdom
> Which has specific knowledge of it,
> To the mother of the Conquerors
> Past, present and future I pay homage.

Here "inconceivable" and "inexpressible" mean that reality cannot be apprehended by conceptual thought or described as it is experienced by exalted beings. The space-like mere negation or absence of inherent existence is unproduced and does not disintegrate or cease. The exalted wisdom which apprehends it is a perfection of wisdom because it takes us beyond cyclic existence. Emptiness, the absence of inherent existence, is apprehended as it is by no other cognition except this exalted wisdom which acts as a mother, giving birth to the enlightened beings of the past, present and future.

We have considered here how one engages with suchness from the point of view of personal practice, by first recognizing suffering, identifying its source, realizing that cessation of suffering is possible and cultivating the path of understanding reality which leads to this. Establishing the selflessness of "I" and "mine" enables us to overcome the false view of the transitory collection from which springs the grasping that keeps us in cyclic existence. Next we will consider how ordinary and exalted beings apprehend reality.

By gradual steps the Buddha led those he taught to drink the nectar[54] of the correct view. At the beginning he presented things in conformity with the way they are conventionally perceived. He did not emphasize that the aggregates, elements and sources change moment by moment but taught only about the coarse impermanence of the continuum, since the apparent changes that take place can be observed by everyone. Only later did he speak about the constant change all products undergo. To worldly perception these things are real in that they seem stable, but to the perception of exalted beings they are all false, appearing to be stable when they are actually in constant flux.

Then, when the student was sufficiently prepared, the Buddha taught that since all bases are free from existence by way of their own entity, it is inappropriate to distinguish between them by specifying that some are real and others are not. Discussion of whether a rabbit's horn is long or short is meaningless, since a rabbit's horn has no existence in the first place.

The importance of leading the student to the nectar of suchness is stressed, but what is suchness or ultimate truth? Ultimate truth as perceived by the exalted ones has five defining features.[55] It is that which "cannot be known through another," since it can only be directly understood as it is by uncontaminated exalted wisdom and not through others' descriptions or other states of mind.

Anything a person suffering from a certain eye disease looks at seems to be covered with hairs. Even if someone with good sight reassures him that there are no hairs present, he will not see what he is looking at in the way that the person with good sight sees it. Nevertheless, although the hairs still continue to appear, the information he has received helps him to understand that the hairs merely appear but do not actually exist and that the fault lies with his vision.

Similarly, though ordinary people do not perceive reality in the way exalted beings do, they can with the help of the teachings understand that though things appear to be inherently existent, they are actually empty of such existence. Their understanding arises by way of a mental image.

Just as the person suffering from the eye disease cannot see things without the appearance of hairs but can know there are no hairs present, ordinary people cannot see things without duality[56] yet can understand emptiness.

124 The Six Perfections

When the person with the eye disease applies the right eye ointment, he can cure the ailment completely and see with good sight. Now the hairs no longer appear and the person knows with certainty that they never existed at all. By applying the eye ointment of a correct understanding of emptiness, the eye condition of ignorance is removed, giving rise to uncontaminated understanding which sees suchness without any fabrications.

Pacification is the second defining characteristic of ultimate truth. Without the eye disease hairs do not appear. Similarly without the influence of ignorance, it is clear that things are actually pacified of or free from existence by way of their own entity. This cannot be expressed or described as it is by language which elaborates the diversity of things and in this respect the ultimate is inexpressible. A contrast is made here between the unified fundamental nature of ultimate truth as perceived by direct cognition and the differentiated diversity of conventional phenomena as apprehended by conceptuality and expressed by language.

Ultimate truth is non-conceptual since all movement of conceptuality ceases when it is apprehended directly. It is undifferentiated in that the emptiness of one thing is not a different entity from the emptiness of another.

Nagarjuna speaks about the relationship between emptiness and dependent arising. The great Tsongkhapa's relationship with Manjushri, the embodiment of enlightened wisdom, was one of student and teacher. Manjushri impressed upon Tsongkhapa that emptiness should not be valued over dependent arising and that, if anything, dependent arising should be given even more importance than emptiness.

In his commentary on Chandrakirti's *Supplement to the Middle Way*[57] Tsongkhapa says that although the teachings on emptiness should ideally only be imparted to truly receptive students who, when reality is mentioned, are moved by a sense of great joy, experience goose-pimples and feel tears prick their eyes, students who do not respond in this way but who do not go against their spiritual teacher's instructions will quickly accumulate the merit needed to understand emptiness.

Tsongkhapa points out that if students are not fully ready and receptive, the teacher must take care to insure that they do not misunderstand emptiness nor espouse a nihilistic view. For this reason the fact that things arise dependently and exist in dependence upon causes and conditions and on imputation is emphasized repeatedly.

In *Yogic Deeds of Bodhisattvas* Aryadeva says:

> The conjunction of a listener,
> What is to be heard and an exponent
> Is very rare. In brief, the cycle of
> Rebirths neither has nor has not an end.

When three factors—students who are ready, the authentic teachings and properly qualified teachers—come together, liberation becomes feasible, but not if any of these three essential components is missing.

Nagarjuna's text also considers how ultimate truth is apprehended through inference by ordinary beings. An effect and the cause from which it comes are not inherently one entity. If they were, that which produces and that which is produced would not be different. The cause would be permanent, but in fact it is not, since it changes and turns into the result. Its evolution and continuity preclude its permanence.

Cause and effect are also not inherently different because in that case the effect could not depend on its cause and would be causeless. Since the result comes from the cause, there is no discontinuity. Things therefore are free from the extremes of permanence and annihilation, but occupy a central position in that they lack inherent existence yet have conventional existence.

Ordinary people can understand emptiness through the reason of dependent arising. A sprout has no inherent existence because it arises in dependence on causes and conditions. The sprout is not one with the seed that produces it. If it were, the seed should be present with the sprout, but the seed undergoes change to produce the sprout. The seed and sprout are different but not inherently different, which they would necessarily be if the seed and sprout existed as they appear, namely as findable entities. Inherent difference would preclude relatedness. In that case the continuum of the seed would be broken and the seed would simply discontinue. These features, which are relatively easy to understand with regard to a seed and a sprout, apply to everything which comes into existence through causes and conditions.

Not only products but everything existent is dependent on parts. If a thing and its parts were inherently one, there could be no possessor of the parts and that which is possessed. However, they are also not inherently different because if they were, it should be possible to isolate a thing from its parts.

Dependent arising eliminates both the extreme of permanence and the extreme of annihilation. Since things are "dependent" on their parts, they are not independent and have no inherent, reified or permanent existence. Since they "arise," they are not conventionally non-existent. Their dependent existence precludes existence from their own side.

Furthermore, everything that exists does so through the presence of a basis of designation and the designation. These two are also not inherently one nor inherently different. By thinking about their dependent existence we can understand their lack of inherent existence. Once we have understood this, we must put our understanding into practice.

The Buddha is a refuge to the refugeless and a protector to the protectorless because his nectar-like teaching on the nature of reality gives us the strength to conquer the demonic forces of ordinary death, the contaminated body, the disturbing emotions and the son of the gods, who manifests in the form of interferences that stop us from getting rid of the other demonic forces. The Buddha's teaching clarifies the extremely profound and demonstrates the absence of four impossible kinds of existence: inherent oneness, inherent difference, reified existence and annihilation. By gaining knowledge of this through studying, reflecting and meditating one overcomes birth, sickness, ageing and death, but this nectar and panacea for our ills cannot help us unless we drink it. It is meaningless to praise its marvelous qualities to others if we make no use of it ourselves.

Hearers listen, think and meditate and in that very lifetime, by employing the three kinds of training in ethical discipline, meditative stabilization and wisdom, gain liberation by vanquishing the foe of the disturbing emotions. Many who heard teachings on the nature of reality from the Buddha became Foe Destroyers before they died. Others who received the teaching did not become Foe Destroyers then, yet their practice was not fruitless, for they were able to attain this state in another life.

How could they become Foe Destroyers unless they met with teachers and the teaching in a later life? Even without the presence of enlightened beings as teachers, without the companionship of Hearers and without access to the teachings these practitioners reached the state of Foe Destroyer as Solitary Realizers because of the imprints they had established. For instance, they may have come across a pile of human bones, which caused them to reflect on death and on how it is the consequence of birth. Retracing the process that produced the bones may have activated imprints leading them to contemplate in forward and reverse sequence the twelve-part process through which one remains in cyclic existence.

Developing the understanding of reality through hearing, thinking and meditating is not only vital for those seeking personal liberation but also for practitioners of the Great Vehicle. The wisdom understanding reality is like a sighted guide capable of leading the otherwise blind practices of giving, ethical conduct, patience, enthusiastic effort and concentration to the great city of supreme enlightenment. Wisdom transforms them into perfections that take one beyond both cyclic existence and solitary peace.

Their profound understanding of reality and their ability to see everything as being like a reflection enables Bodhisattvas to give even their flesh without pain or dismay, as calmly as if they were cutting up a medicinal plant. Seeing the extremes of worldly existence and of solitary peace as sources of decline, they observe impeccably the ethical discipline of restraint from harmful activity without the slightest trace of self-interest, which differentiates their practice of ethics from that of others.

With full awareness of the benefits of patience and the drawbacks of impatience, they remain undiscouraged even when their kindness is repaid with ingratitude and hostility, and because of their profound understanding they willingly accept the hardships encountered in their work for others. Without their intelligence and discernment, which shows them the best course of action to pursue with enthusiastic effort, they might waste valuable energy on futile enterprises.

Through lack of understanding we easily become addicted to luxury and sensual pleasure, but Bodhisattvas know how to use such things for their own and others' true well-being. We cling obsessively to those we find lovable, while Bodhisattvas, who have affection for all living beings, because of their profound wisdom are able to love without possessiveness. These wonderful qualities are the result of compassion allied to deep insight into the nature of reality.

In *Yogic Deeds of Bodhisattvas* Aryadeva says:

> Correct perception [leads to] the supreme state,
> Some perception to good rebirths.
> The wise thus always expand their intelligence
> To think about the inner nature.

By knowing reality directly we eventually reach the supreme state of enlightenment, but even a little knowledge of it derived from studying the teachings and reflecting on them can help us attain a good rebirth. Aryadeva thus advises all with intelligence to meditate on the nature of the self.

The various great texts on the Middle Way differ regarding the order in which they present the salient points to be considered in relation to reality. However, if you wish to investigate the nature of reality yourself, you cannot do better than to follow the steps described by Nagarjuna in his *Treatise on the Middle Way*. First become conversant with them and then implement them.

In explaining Nagarjuna's words I have used Tsongkhapa's great commentary in whose validity I have full confidence, but there are many other eminent commentaries on Nagarjuna's *Treatise on the Middle Way*. In the great monastic universities of Tibet, Madhyamika was studied day and night for four years. We learned certain basic texts by heart, studied the great commentaries on them and constantly tested our understanding in debate, but even at the end of that intense period of study no one would ever have claimed to have a perfect understanding of Madhyamika.

It was the tradition in those great monasteries that the sound of the Buddha's teachings was never allowed to die. When ritual assemblies were not being held, debates or recitation were taking place. I was about to attend an all-night debate on Madhyamika when the Chinese troops began bombing Sera and we were forced to flee Tibet, but happily I had the opportunity to continue my studies in India.

Ours is a truly fortunate situation, since we enjoy most of the external and internal conditions that favor spiritual development. We have access to the teachings and to authentic teachers who willingly transmit them to us with compassion and enthusiasm. If understanding of the teachings could be poured into us, they would surely do it. This situation and our own health and strength are fortunate circumstances which can change between morning and evening. Therefore, making an ethical life-style the basis of your practice, take the teachings to heart by hearing, thinking and meditating on them to gain an understanding not only of the words but of their deeper meaning and make effort to discover the nature of reality. Nagarjuna's purpose was to encourage this. Tsongkhapa's *Summary of the Stages of the Path* says:

> Wisdom is the eye for seeing profound suchness,
> It is the path which totally uproots worldly existence
> And the treasure of knowledge praised in all the scriptures,
> Renowned as the finest lamp
> To dispel the darkness of confusion.
> Knowing this, the wise who seek liberation
> Cultivate this path with every effort.

APPENDIX

The Eighteenth Chapter of Nagarjuna's *Treatise on the Middle Way*

Each of Nagarjuna's verses is followed by a brief explanation based on Tsongkhapa's commentary *Ocean of Reasoning*.

1   **If the aggregates were the self**
    It would be produced and disintegrate.
    If it were different from the aggregates
    It would lack the aggregates' characteristics.

If the aggregates and the self were intrinsically one and totally identical, the self would be produced and disintegrate just like the aggregates. In that case the self would be inseparable from the aggregates of this life and when they cease, it also would cease. Like the aggregates of this life the self would have come into existence and been newly produced at birth and would therefore not be beginningless. If the aggregates were the self, there should either be only one aggregate, since there is only one self, or five selves because there are five aggregates—forms, feelings, discriminations, compositional factors and consciousnesses.

If the self were intrinsically different from the aggregates, the features of production, duration and disintegration, which distinguish the aggregates as products, would not pertain to the self, just as the features of a cow, such as its horns, do not pertain to an unrelated animal such as a horse. In that case the self should be a non-product like nirvana or a sky flower.

If the self were inherently distinct from the individual characteristics of the five aggregates, it should be found when all the aggregates have been eliminated and would be apprehensible as an entity distinct from the aggregates, just as form can be apprehended as an entity distinct from mind.

2   If the self has no existence,
     How can the self's have any existence?
     Since the self and the self's are pacified
     Conceptions of the "I" and "mine" cease.

If the self has no existence by way of its own nature, how could that which is the self's exist by way of its own entity? By meditating on their lack of intrinsic existence, one comes to a direct experience of their emptiness. At that time all appearances of the self, the object of misconceptions of the "I," and of the aggregates, the object of misconceptions of "mine," are pacified. Namely, to the mind in direct meditative equipoise on emptiness neither the self nor the aggregates appear because the perceiving awareness, the subject, and emptiness, the object, have become one taste. Through this all conceptions of an inherently existent "I" and "mine" will eventually cease, since the correct understanding of reality and the misconception that must be eliminated are diametrically opposed in their mode of apprehension. The one engages with reality as it is while the other distorts reality.

3   Those with no conceptions
     Of "I" and "mine" also have no existence.
     Whoever sees those who lack conceptions
     Of "I" and "mine" does not see.

Meditators who have rid themselves of conceptions of an "I" and "mine" themselves lack existence by way of their own entity. Someone who sees those who have rid themselves of these misconceptions as existing by way of their own entity will not see suchness nor eliminate his or her own misconceptions.

4   When ideas of both the inner and outer
     As the self and the self's come to an end,
     Grasping will be stopped
     And through its ending birth will end.

When ideas of the inner and of the outer[58] as a self and the self's in terms of true existence cease, grasping, the ninth link in the twelve-part process which keeps us within cyclic existence, will stop. Such grasping is directed towards what is desired, views, systems of ethical discipline and conduct, and the self. When grasping ends, birth in cyclic existence through contaminated actions comes to an end.

5   Liberation is won by ending actions and afflictions—
     Actions and afflictions come from thoughts.
     Those arise from fabrications.
     Fabrications are stopped by emptiness.

Liberation comes about by ending contaminated actions underlain by disturbing emotions. When grasping, which is a disturbing emotion, ends, existence, which is the tenth link in the twelve-part process and classed as action, does not occur. In this way involuntary birth and death cease. Actions arise from disturbing emotions. Disturbing emotions arise from the thoughts associated with an incorrect mental approach which exaggerates attractiveness and unattractiveness. The thoughts which constitute an incorrect mental approach arise from our familiarity with seeing things as truly existent. These fabrications of true existence cease when we gain familiarity with the emptiness of the things on which these fabrications focus.

6   They have declared the self exists
    And also taught the self does not exist.
    Buddhas moreover have taught that neither
    The self nor selflessness have any existence.

In order to make those in danger of performing serious mis-
deeds that would lead to bad rebirths more careful, Buddhas
have declared that the self has real existence. They have taught
those engaged in virtue but tightly enmeshed in conceptions
of true existence that there is no self in order to loosen their
adherence to false views of the transitory collection. To those
who have gained much familiarity with virtue and who are
receptive and capable of understanding the profound nature
of reality they have taught that neither the self nor selflessness has any intrinsic existence.

7   The subject-matter is non-existent
    Since the mind's sphere is non-existent.
    Unproduced and unceasing,
    Reality is like nirvana.

If anything had intrinsic existence it would have been indicated by the enlightened ones, but they have not mentioned
any ultimately existent subject-matter or ultimately existent
expression of it by language, for such ultimate existence is
not a sphere of activity of the mind.[59] The unproduced and
unceasing reality of all phenomena is like nirvana. Nirvana
is the pacification of all fabrications. Meditation on the
unproduced and unceasing reality of all phenomena leads to
a state in which all fabrications of true existence are pacified.
Moreover, for the mind engaged in direct perception of reality during meditative equipoise all fabrications are pacified.

8   The Buddha taught that everything
    Is real, not real,
    Both real and unreal,
    And neither unreal nor real.

To those who through the imprints of conceptions of true existence see both the container, the physical environment, and the contents, the living beings within it, as trustworthy, enduring and not disintegrating until their final moment, the Buddha taught in accordance with conventional appearance that they are real. He did this to arouse their confidence in his teaching. To overcome even subtle conceptions of permanence in those who realize that things could not exist in this way he taught that they are not real but deceptive because they actually undergo constant change, although they seem to remain unchanged.

They are both real and unreal, since to the perception of ordinary childlike people these things appear to be real, in the sense of unchanging, while to the perception of exalted beings in the period following meditative equipoise on reality they appear to be unreal and deceptive. For those who have had previous familiarity with emptiness, but who in this life hold conceptions of true existence due to the influence of philosophical tenets, he taught that both the things which are perceived as unreal or impermanent and those which appear to be real or permanent have no existence by way of their own entity.[60]

9   **It is not known through others,**
      Is pacified, not elaborated
      By elaborations and is without
      Conceptuality and differentness.
      These are the characteristics of suchness.

The ultimate has five features. It can only be experienced as it is by one's own uncontaminated exalted wisdom and cannot be known by other means, since it cannot be described or conceptualized as it actually is. It is pacified in that it is free from any nature of existence by way of its own entity. Thought and speech distinguish the diversity of things but such elaborations do not apply to emptiness. When reality is experienced directly all conceptuality stops. There are no differences between the emptiness of one thing and the emptiness of others.

10   **Whatever arises relying on something else**
      Is from the outset not that.
      Nor is it other than that.
      Thus it is neither non-existent nor permanent.

An effect which arises by depending on a cause is not inherently one with that cause, nor is it inherently different from that cause. If it were inherently one with its cause, that which is produced and the producer would absurdly be one. The effect would already exist at the time of the cause, which would be permanent. If the effect were inherently different from its cause, it could not depend upon it nor come into existence through it and the continuum of the cause would cease. Since the cause transforms into the effect, it is not permanent. Since the continuum of the cause persists in the form of the effect, it does not become non-existent nor discontinue.

11   **The nectar taught by the Buddhas,**
      Who are the world's protectors,
      Is that things are not one nor different,
      Neither non-existent nor permanent.

The teachings of the Buddhas clarify the nectar-like profound nature of suchness which removes the suffering of birth, ageing, sickness and death. The Buddhas are the world's protectors because they befriend the friendless, support the helpless and protect the protectorless. They teach that dependently arising nominally imputed phenomena are neither inherently one with nor inherently different from their causes and conditions or parts and that their mode of existence is between the two extremes in that they are neither totally non-existent nor do they have any reified existence.

12   Even when fully enlightened Buddhas
      Are not present and there are no more Hearers,
      The exalted wisdom of Solitary Realizers
      Comes into being without any reliance.

Some Hearers listen to the teachings of an enlightened being and through their practice of ethical discipline, concentration and wisdom become Foe Destroyers in the same life. Others do so in a later life when the imprints created through hearing, thinking and meditating are awakened by the advent of an enlightened being or spiritual teacher. But what if this does not happen? Even when no enlightened beings manifest in the world and there are no longer any Hearers to act as spiritual guides, the exalted wisdom of Solitary Realizers will arise without depending on a teacher because of the strength of past imprints and as a result of the great merit they have accumulated.

This concludes the eighteenth chapter, analyzing the self and other phenomena.

THE TIBETAN TEXT

The Eighteenth Chapter of
The Treatise on the Middle Way

by
Nagarjuna

༡ གལ་ཏེ་ཕྱུང་པོ་བདག་ཨིན་ན།
སྐྱི་དང་འཛིག་པ་ཅན་དུ་འགྱུར།
གལ་ཏེ་ཕྱུང་པོ་རྣམས་ལས་གཞན།
ཕྱུང་པོའི་མཚན་ཉིད་མེད་པར་འགྱུར།

༢ བདག་ཉིད་ཡོད་པ་མ་ཨིན་ན།
བདག་གི་ཡོད་པར་ག་ལ་འགྱུར།
བདག་དང་བདག་གི་ཞི་བའི་ཕྱིར།
ངར་འཛིན་ང་ཡིར་འཛིན་མེད་འགྱུར།

༣ ངར་འཛིན་ང་ཡིར་འཛིན་མེད་གང་།
དེ་ཡང་ཡོད་པ་མ་ཡིན་ཏེ།
ངར་འཛིན་ང་ཡིར་འཛིན་མེད་པར།
གང་གིས་མཐོང་བས་མི་མཐོང་རོ།

༩ ནད་དང་ཁྱི་རོ་ལ་ཉིད་དགའ་ལ།
བདག་དང་བདག་གི་སྐམ་ཟད་ན།
ཉེ་བར་ལེན་པ་འགགས་འགྱུར་ཞིང་།
དེ་ཟད་པས་ན་སྐྱེ་བ་ཟད།

༥ ལས་དང་ཉོན་མོངས་ཟད་པས་ཐར།
ལས་དང་ཉོན་མོངས་རྣམ་རྟོག་ལས།
དེ་དག་སྤྲོས་ལས་སྤྲོས་པ་ནི།
སྟོང་པ་ཉིད་ཀྱིས་འགགས་པར་འགྱུར།

༦ བདག་གོ་ཞེས་ཀྱང་བཏགས་གྱུར་ཅིང་།
བདག་མེད་ཅེས་ཀྱང་བསྟན་པར་གྱུར།
སངས་རྒྱས་རྣམས་ཀྱིས་བདག་དང་ནི།
བདག་མེད་འགའང་མེད་ཅེས་ཀྱང་བསྟན།

༧ བརྗོད་པར་བྱ་བ་ལྡོག་པ་སྟེ།
སེམས་ཀྱི་སྤྱོད་ཡུལ་ལྡོག་པས་སོ།
མ་སྐྱེས་པ་དང་མ་འགགས་པ།
ཆོས་ཉིད་མྱ་ངན་འདས་དང་མཚུངས།

༩ ཐམས་ཅད་ཡང་དག་ཡང་དག་མིན།
ཡང་དག་ཡང་དག་མ་ཡིན་ཉིད།
ཡང་དག་མིན་མིན་ཡང་དག་མིན།
དེ་ནི་སངས་རྒྱས་རྗེས་བསྟན་པའོ།

༯ གཞན་ལས་ཤེས་མིན་ཞི་བ་དང་།
སྤྲོས་པ་རྣམས་ཀྱིས་མ་སྤྲོས་པ།
རྣམ་རྟོག་མེད་དོན་ཐ་དད་མེད།
དེ་ནི་དེ་ཉིད་མཚན་ཉིད་དོ།

༡༠ གང་ལ་བརྟེན་ཏེ་གང་བྱུང་བ།
དེ་ནི་རེ་ཤིག་དེ་ཉིད་མིན།
དེ་ལས་གཞན་པའང་མ་ཡིན་པ།
དེ་ཕྱིར་ཆད་མིན་རྟག་མ་ཡིན།

༡༡ སངས་རྒྱས་འཇིག་རྟེན་མགོན་རྣམས་ཀྱི།
བསྟན་པ་བདུད་རྩིར་གྱུར་པ་དེ།
དོན་གཅིག་མ་ཡིན་ཐ་དད་མིན།
ཆད་པ་མ་ཡིན་རྟག་མ་ཡིན།

༡༢   རྟོག་གས་སངས་རྒྱས་རྣམས་མ་བྱུང་ཞིང་།

ཉན་ཐོས་རྣམས་ནི་ཟད་གྱུར་ཀྱང་།

རང་སངས་རྒྱས་ཀྱི་ཡེ་ཤེས་ནི།

བརྟེན་པ་མེད་ལས་རབ་ཏུ་སྐྱེ།

བདག་བཏག་པ་ཞེས་བྱ་བ་སྟེ་རབ་ཏུ་བྱེད་པ་བཅོ་བརྒྱད་པའོ།།

Notes

Abbreviation:

P: *Tibetan Tripiṭaka* (Tokyo-Kyoto: Tibetan Tripitaka Research Foundation, 1956)

1. Maitreya's *Ornament for the Mahayana Sutras* (*Mahāyānasūtrā-laṃkāra, Theg pa chen po'i mdo sde'i rgyan*, P5521, Vol. 108) consists of twenty-one chapters which deal mainly with Mahayana conduct and present the Chittamatrin view. The text seeks to establish the authenticity of the Mahayana sutras as the words of the Buddha. When the Buddha Shakyamuni came to our world from the Tushita pure land (dGa' ldan yid dga' chos 'dzin) Maitreya took over as its spiritual ruler. He will eventually manifest in this world as the next Buddha and display the deeds of a supreme emanation body (*mchog gi sprul sku*). It is said that if one hears and thinks about the five treatises which he revealed to Asanga, one will be reborn in the Tushita pure land. In Tibet many of the largest statues were of Maitreya, who is represented sitting on a throne with his feet on the ground, ready to rise and come into the world. Just as Avalokiteshvara is the embodiment of compassion, Maitreya is the embodiment of love.

The seventeenth chapter of his *Ornament for the Mahayana Sutras* explains how the six perfections are the foundation for one's own temporary and ultimate well-being and the foundation for others' well-being, how they include all Mahayana paths of practice, how each develops from the preceding one and what the practice of each promotes.

2. Tsongkhapa (Tsong kha pa Blo bzang grags pa, 1357-1419), born in Amdo (A mdo), was a great reformer, dedicated practitioner and prolific writer. He founded Ganden Monastery (dGa' ldan rnam par rgyal ba'i gling) in 1409, the first of the monastic universities of the new Kadampa (bKa' gdams gsar ma) or Gelugpa (dGe lugs pa) tradition. His *Great Exposition of the Stages of the Path* (*Lam rim chen mo*, P6001, Vol. 152) and his other works on the stages of the path were directly inspired by the Indian master Atisha's practice-oriented *Lamp for the Path to Enlightenment* (*Bodhipathapradipa, Byang chub lam gyi sgron ma*, P5343, Vol. 103).

3. The Indian Buddhist master Nagarjuna (Klu sgrub, first to second century) was the trailblazer who established the Madhyamika system of philosophical tenets. In the *Precious Garland of Advice for the King* (*Rājaparikathāratnāvalī, rGyal po la gtam bya ba rin po che'i phreng ba*, P5658, Vol. 129) Nagarjuna explains both the extensive and profound paths to enlightenment, emphasizing that the root of enlightenment is the exalted understanding of reality. The text was addressed to his friend, a king of the Satavahana dynasty which ruled over a vast area of India including much of modern Madhya Pradesh, Maharashtra, Andhra Pradesh, part of south Orissa and part of Karnataka. In Tibetan literature this king is referred to by the name of bDe spyod bzang po. The *Precious Garland* contains very practical advice, still relevant today, on how to govern in accordance with the Buddha's teaching. English translation in: Jeffrey Hopkins, *Buddhist Advice for Living & Liberation: Nāgārjuna's Precous Garland* (Ithaca: Snow Lion Publications, 1998).

4. The Tibetan *pha rol tu chin pa* is normally translated as "perfection." *Pha rol* means "beyond," while *chin pa* means "gone."

5. Hearers (*snyan thos*) and Solitary Realizers (*rang sangs rgyas*) are intent on gaining personal liberation. They are practitioners of the Hinayana or Lesser Vehicle (*theg dman pa*), so called because their objective is limited to their own well-being. Practitioners of the Mahayana or Great Vehicle (*theg chen pa*), also referred to as practitioners of the Bodhisattva Vehicle, aspire to attain complete enlightenment for the sake of all beings and therefore have a greater objective. Solitary Realizers accumulate more merit over a longer period than Hearers and do not depend upon the instructions of a spiritual teacher in their last rebirth before they attain liberation and become Foe Destroyers. Foe Destroyers (*dgra bcom pa*) are those who have vanquished the foe of the disturbing emotions and put an end to their cyclic existence by uprooting ignorance.

6. Tsongkhapa attributes the quotation to the *Moonlight Sutra* (*Zla ba sgron ma'i mdo*). This name refers to the *King of Meditative Stabilizations Sutra* (*Sarvadharmasvabhāvasamatāvipañcitasamādhirājasūtra, Ting nge 'dzin rgyal po mdo*, P795, Vols. 31-32), in which the Buddha frequently addresses a youth called Moonlight. The cited passage is addressed to Ananda in the thirty-sixth chapter of the sutra. Tsongkhapa's version shows minor variants from the present text of the sutra.

7. The Indian master Shantideva lived in the monastic university of Nalanda during the eighth century. To others he appeared quite unaccomplished and they said he only knew three things: how to eat, sleep and defecate. In an attempt to humiliate him he was designated to teach before a large gathering. To everyone's amazement he showed himself to be a very great master by teaching his guide to the Bodhisattva's way of life, *Engaging in the Bodhisattvas Deeds* (*Bodhisattva-caryāvatāra, Byang chub sems dpa'i spyod pa la 'jug pa*, P5272, Vol. 99) and by displaying miraculous feats. The work mentioned here, the *Compendium of Training* (*Śikṣāsamuccaya, bSlabs pa kun las btus pa*, P5272, Vol. 102), is a compilation and elucidation of sutra passages about the training of Bodhisattvas. English translation in: Shantideva, *The Way of the Bodhisattva*, translated from the Tibetan by the Padmakara Translation Group (Boston: Shambhala, 1997).

8. Aryadeva was the spiritual son of Nagarjuna and was active in the monastic university of Nalanda during the first half of the third century. His work *Four Hundred Stanzas on the Yogic Deeds of Bodhisattvas* (*Bodhisattvayogacaryācatuḥśatakaśāstra, Byang chub sems dpa'i rnal 'byor spyod pa bzhi brgya pa'i bstan bcos*, P5246, Vol. 95) discusses the distorted ideas and disturbing emotions which prevent true Bodhisattva activity and the attainment of enlightenment. The first eight chapters establish conventional reality, while the second eight establish ultimate reality by refuting various misconceptions regarding, for instance, the person, time, space and matter. English translation in: Geshe Sonam Rinchen and Ruth Sonam, *Yogic Deeds of Bodhisattvas: Gyeltsap on Aryadeva's Four Hundred* (Ithaca: Snow Lion Publications, 1994).

9. *Dharmasaṃgītisūtra, Chos yang dag par sdud pa'i mdo*, P904, Vol. 36.

10. The Indian master Atisha (982-1054) was born into a royal family probably in what is now Bengal. Owing to his parents' opposition he had difficulty disengaging himself from royal life, but eventually, after a number of attempts, succeeded and became ordained. He studied with a hundred and fifty-seven spiritual masters but was always very moved when he recalled Dharmakirti of Suvarnadvipa, the master of the

Golden Isles. Atisha made a perilous thirteen-month sea journey to Indonesia to study with this master, with whom he remained for twelve years and to whom he attributed his development of the altruistic intention. After his return to India he lived in the monastic university of Vikramashila, from where he was invited to Tibet. He remained in Tibet from 1042 until his death and his teaching activity there had a profound influence on the development of Buddhism in that country.

11. Dromtön Gyelway Jungnay ('Brom ston rGyal ba'i 'byung gnas, 1004-1064), the main Tibetan disciple of the Indian master Atisha, was a lay practitioner and held lay-person's vows. He was the founder of the Kadampa (bKa' gdams pa) tradition.

12. *Lam rim bsdus don / Byang chub lam gyi rim pa'i nyams len gyi rnam gzhag mdor bsdus*, *The Collected Works of Rje Tson-kha-pa Blo-bzan-gragspa*, Vol. kha, *thor bu*, 65b.2-68b.1 (New Delhi: Ngawang Gelek Demo, 1975–). For an English translation of the verses by Ruth Sonam, see "The Abridged Stages of the Path to Enlightenment" in *Chö Yang* No. 7 (Sidhpur: Norbulingka Institute, 1996).

13. Nagarjuna's *Letter to a Friend* (*Suhṛllekha*, *bShes pa'i spring yig*, P5682, Vol. 129), like his *Precious Garland*, addresses advice to his friend the king of the Satavahana dynasty. It discusses concisely and in detail the practices associated with the three different levels of capacity and is directed towards both householders and the ordained.

14. Geshe Potowa (Po to ba Rin chen gsal, 1031-1105), Geshe Chengawa (sPyan snga ba Tshul khrims 'bar, 1038-1103) and Geshe Puchungwa (Phu chung ba gZhon nu rgyal mtshan, 1031-1106), known as the three Kadampa brothers, were the spiritual heirs of Dromtön Gyelway Jungnay, the founder of the Kadampa tradition. Geshe Langritangpa (Glang ri thang pa, 1054-1123) wrote the *Eight Verses for Training the Mind* (*Blo sbyong tshig brgyad ma*), which inspired a number of other texts in the mind training (*blo sbyong*) tradition for which the Kadampa masters are famed. One of these, the *Seven Points for Training the Mind* (*Blo sbyong don bdun ma*), was written as a result of its author Geshe Chekawa's (mChad kha ba, 1101-1175) wish to discover more about the meaning of Geshe Langritangpa's words, "May I accept the loss and offer the victory to others." He received the teaching from Geshe Sharawa (Shar ra ba, also known as Shar ba pa, 1070-1141), since by that time Geshe Langritangpa had already passed away. These masters were known for their pithy down-to-earth approach to practice, which they presented according to the three levels of capacity clearly explained in Atisha's *Lamp for the Path to Enlightenment*. They emphasized the practice of sutra and kept their personal practice of tantra hidden.

15. Geshe Bengungyel ('Ban gung rgyal), one of the Kadampa masters, had been a thief and brigand earlier in his life. Later, after he had reformed, he used to chide himself when he noticed that he was doing or thinking anything unwholesome. He would say, "There you go again, you villain Bengungyel, still at your old ways!" But when he had done or thought something good, he would use his religious name and say, "Congratulations, Geshe Tsultrim Gyelwa, keep up the good work!"

16. "Those of the nine states" (*skye rgu* or *skye dgu*) is frequently used to denote all living beings. "Nine states" refers to those born into the desire realm from the desire, form and formless realms; those born into the form realm from the desire, form and formless realms and those born into the formless realm from the desire, form and formless realms.

17. The Indian Buddhist master Chandrakirti was the main spiritual son of Nagarjuna, whose works on sutra and tantra he elucidated and propagated. He lived in the monastic university of Nalanda during the seventh century and was an accomplished practitioner. Chandrakirti's *Supplement to the Middle Way* (*Madhyamakāvatāra, dBu ma la 'jug pa*, P5261, P5262, Vol. 98) is a commentary on the meaning of Nagarjuna's *Treatise on the Middle Way*, which it supplements with regard to the extensive aspect of practice. It deals with the ten Bodhisattva stages.

18. *Bodhisattvayogacaryācatuḥśatakaṭīkā, Byang chub sems dpa'i rnal 'byor spyod pa bzhi brgya pa'i rgya cher 'grel pa*, P5266, Vol. 98.

19. The garuda (*bya khyung*) is a mythical and extremely powerful eagle-like bird, the legendary foe of snakes and serpentine creatures called nagas.

20. The three kinds of enthusiastic effort are armor-like enthusiastic effort (*go cha'i brtson 'grus*), the enthusiastic effort of creating virtue (*dge ba'i chos sdud kyi brtson 'grus*) and the enthusiastic effort of working for living beings (*sems can don byed kyi brtson 'grus*).

21. The *Three Principal Aspects of the Path* (*Lam gyi gtso bo rnam gsum*, P6087, Vol. 153) is a short prayer outlining the essential points associated with the three principal attitudes and insights which form the basis for the practice of sutra and tantra: the wish to gain freedom from cyclic existence, the altruistic intention to attain enlightenment for the good of all living beings and the correct understanding of reality. English translation in Geshe Lhundup Sopa and Jeffrey Hopkins, *Cutting through Appearances: Practice and Theory of Tibetan Buddhism* (Ithaca: Snow Lion Publications, 1989).

22. The five extremely grave actions (*mtshams med lnga*), which lead straight to a bad rebirth without any intervening (*mtshams med pa*) life,

are killing one's mother, father, or a Foe Destroyer, causing schism within the spiritual community, and drawing blood from the body of a Buddha with the intention to harm. The five almost as grave actions (*nye ba'i mtshams med lnga*), which also lead straight to a bad rebirth, are incest with one's mother if she is a Foe Destroyer, murdering a Bodhisattva, murdering an exalted being of the Lesser Vehicle, stealing what belongs to the spiritual community and destroying a monastery or reliquary monument out of hatred.

23. The *Sutra Encouraging the Special Wish* (*Adhyāśayasamcodanasūtra, lHag pa'i bsam pa bskul pa'i mdo*) forms the twenty-fifth chapter of the *Heap of Jewels Sutra* (*Mahāratnakūtadharmaparyāyaśatasāhasrikagranthasūtra, dKon mchog brtsegs pa chen po'i chos kyi rnam grangs le'u stong phrag brgya pa'i mdo*, P760, Vols. 22-24).

24. Drukpa Kunlek ('Brug pa kun legs, 1455-1529) was an itinerant Kagyu (bKa' brgyud) master whose direct trenchant remarks and eccentric behavior shocked others out of their complacency and caused them to practice with greater sincerity. Tales of his exploits are still beloved today.

25. This image of the Buddha (referred to as the *rJo bo* or Lord) was considered the most precious image in the whole of Tibet. It is said to have been made during the Buddha's lifetime. From India it was taken to China and later brought to Tibet by King Srongtsen Gampo's (Srong brtsan sgam po) Chinese wife in the middle of the seventh century. Ordained and lay-people throughout Tibet aspired to make a pilgrimage to see this image. To do so was considered to be as good as seeing the Buddha himself and receiving his blessings.

26. The four concentrations (*bsam gtan*) or absorptions (*snyoms 'jug*) of the form realm are differentiated on the basis of the accompanying feelings. A progressive development towards neutral feeling takes place. There are seventeen abodes (*gnas*) of the form realm divided among the four concentrations. The four absorptions of the formless realm are called limitless space (*nam mkha' mtha' yas*), limitless consciousness (*rnam shes mtha' yas*), nothingness (*ci yang med*) and the peak of cyclic existence (*srid rtse*). They are differentiated on the basis of the accompanying discrimination, which becomes less and less coarse.

27. Many states of meditative stabilization (*ting nge 'dzin*) are mentioned in sutra. "The continuity of the teachings meditative stabilization" (*chos rgyun gyi ting nge 'dzin*), which allows one constantly to remember the words and meaning of the scriptures without forgetting them, is attained on the third and highest phase of the Mahayana path of

accumulation and is dependent upon the achievement of actual concentration (*bsam gtan*). Four kinds of meditative stabilization are associated with the four seals, which are the basic tenets of Buddhism: that all products are impermanent, that all contaminated things are miserable, that everything existent is empty and selfless and that nirvana is peace. The "wishless meditative stabilization" (*smon pa med pa'i ting nge 'dzin*), focusing on all products as impermanent and all contaminated things as miserable, counters the aspiration to attain anything associated with the three realms of cyclic existence. The "emptiness meditative stabilization" (*stong nyid kyi ting nge 'dzin*) counteracts many different misconceptions regarding the nature of things. The "signless meditative stabilization" (*tshad ma med pa'i ting nge 'dzin*) focuses on nirvana, the state in which all signs of suffering and its causes are pacified. Through directly understanding the illusion-like nature of all dependently arising things the "illusion-like meditative stabilization" (*sgyu ma lta bu'i ting nge 'dzin*) rids one of obstructions to creating manifestations.

Meditative stabilization is essential for the effective practice of the stage of generation in tantra, during which emphasis is placed on gaining clear visualization of the residence and resident deities of the mandala. It is also essential for the practice of the stage of completion, in which the concentration is focused on the energy channels, energy winds and constituents.

28. The five faults (*nyes pa lnga*) or hindrances to the accomplishment of a calmly abiding mind are (1) laziness (*le lo*), (2) forgetfulness (*brjed pa*), also referred to as "forgetting the instructions" (*gdams ngag brjed pa*), (3) slackness (*bying ba*) or excitement (*rgod pa*), (4) not applying antidotes (*mngon par 'du mi byed pa*) when they are needed and (5) applying them (*mngon par 'du byed pa*) unnecessarily.

The eight antidotes (*gnyen po brgyad*) are (1) appreciation of the benefits derived from meditative stabilization (*ting nge 'dzin gyi yon tan mthong ba'i dad pa*), (2) the aspiration to attain meditative stabilization (*ting nge 'dzin don gnyer gyi 'dun pa*), (3) enthusiastic effort in accomplishing meditative stabilization (*ting nge 'dzin rtsol ba'i brtson 'grus*) and (4) pliancy (*shin sbyangs*). These four counteract laziness. Forgetfulness is counteracted by (5) mindfulness (*dran pa*); slackness and excitement are identified by (6) mental alertness (*shes bzhin*); not dealing with them is remedied by (7) applying the proper antidotes (*mngon par 'du byed pa*) and overzealousness is counteracted by (8) not applying antidotes (*mngon par 'du mi byed pa*).

29. These energy centers are part of the subtle body, consisting of energy winds, energy channels and their constituents, on which tantric

practices focus, particularly those associated with the stage of completion. The seed syllables represent certain forces or, in the case of *om, ah, hung,* denote enlightened body, speech and mind. They may also be the seed from which one visualizes a deity arising.

30. Pervasive focal objects (*khyab pa'i dmigs pa*) include non-analytical images (*rnam par mi rtog pa'i gzugs brnyan*) and analytical images (*rnam par rtog pa dang bcas pa'i gzugs brnyan*). These two are posited from the point of view of the subjective awareness observing the focal object. The first refers to the way awareness observes its object during calm abiding practice and the second to how awareness engages with its object during the cultivation of special insight.

The third group, the limits of phenomena (*dngos po'i mtha'*) includes the limit of phenomena in their diversity (*ji snyed pa'i dngos po'i mtha'*) and the limit of phenomena as they are (*ji lta ba'i dngos po'i mtha'*), referring to their final nature. They are so called because all phenomena are contained within these limits and there are none beyond. From the point of view of the wide diversity of phenomena, all products can be included within the five aggregates, all phenomena within the eighteen constituents and twelve sources, and everything which can be known within the four noble truths. All these focal objects have the same final nature, which can be established by reasoning, and none is an exception to this.

The fourth group, thorough achievement of the purpose (*dgos pa yongs su grub pa*), is posited from the point of view of the effect. Through placing one's attention on the image of any object by way of calm abiding and special insight meditation, through continual meditation on the same object, through familiarity and through the power of doing it many times, one becomes free of all hindrances which prevent complete serviceability of body and mind. This explanation is based on the section dealing with focal objects from Je Tsongkhapa's *Great Exposition of the Stages of the Path.*

31. Asanga (Thogs med), an Indian Buddhist master who lived in the fourth century, was a trailblazer in establishing the Chittamatra (*sems tsam*) system of philosophical tenets, although he himself is said to have held the Prasangika-Madhyamika (*dbu ma thal 'gyur pa*) view. His *Compendium of Knowledge* (*Abhidharmasamuccaya, mNgon pa kun btus,* P5550, Vol. 112) sets out the focal objects of the paths: the aggregates, constituents and elements, the four noble truths and the twelve links of dependent arising. An extensive explanation of mind and mental activities is included. The text contains instructions on how to practice by controlling one's senses and training in ethical discipline, concentration and wisdom as well as explanation of the thirty-seven

factors concordant with enlightenment. It concludes by explaining the results of these practices, through which all faults are brought to an end and the highest wisdom is attained. These topics are presented mainly from a Chittamatrin standpoint.

32. The Indian master Kamalashila, a student of Shantarakshita, participated in a decisive debate with a Chinese monk identified as Hvashang Mahayana. This debate was held in Tibet in 792 at Samye Monastery (bSam yas) and, according to Tibetan sources, the outcome definitively settled that Buddhism in Tibet would follow the Indian rather than the Chinese model. Kamalashila's *Stages of Meditation* (*Bhāvanā-krama, sGom pa'i rim pa*, P5310-12, Vol. 102) sets forth his views. It has three parts. The first explains primarily how selflessness is established through hearing and thinking. The second part describes how to meditate on selflessness and the third delineates the results of doing this. Each part stands as a complete work in itself.

33. The preceding passage mentions six recollections (*rjes su dran pa drug*): recollecting the enlightened ones (*sangs rgyas rjes su dran pa*), their teachings (*chos rjes su dran pa*) and the spiritual community (*dge 'dun rjes su dran pa*), recollecting generosity (*sbyin pa rjes su dran pa*), ethical discipline (*tshul khrims rjes su dran pa*) and the gods (*lha rjes su dran pa*). The last may be taken to refer to the fine qualities of celestial beings in the desire and form realms or to the fact that the Buddha is the god of gods, since all worldly gods are said to pay reverence to him.

34. Each of the concentrations of the form and formless realm has seven preparations (*nyer bsdogs*). The first preparation for the first concentration of the form realm is accomplished when calm abiding is attained and its nature is calm abiding. The other six are in the nature of special insight. When the first preparation is attained, the meditator may embark on worldly paths which do not lead beyond cyclic existence, but through which manifest disturbing emotions can be suppressed. These paths involve the contemplation of lower states within cyclic existence as coarse and undesirable and higher states as subtle and thus desirable.

   The first preparation can also act as a basis for uncontaminated paths. This is the direction taken by most Buddhist practitioners, since from a Buddhist point of view it leads to the development of genuine spiritual paths, namely those associated with the wish for freedom from cyclic existence, and to liberation itself. True suffering and true sources of suffering are seen as disadvantageous and coarse, while true cessations and true paths are seen as advantageous and peaceful. As a result one is able eventually to rid oneself completely of the disturbing emotions and their seeds.

35. *Prajñāśatakanāmaprakaraṇa*, *Shes rab brgya ba*, P5820, Vol. 144.

36. The wheel of the teachings (*chos kyi 'khor lo*) consists of the scriptural teachings and their embodiment in the form of insights. The image of a wheel rolling from place to place signifies the process by which the teachings are passed on in a living tradition. The teachings are given and those who receive them practice, gain insights and then, in turn, teach from their own experience. The sharp spokes protruding beyond the rim of the wheel turn it into a weapon which destroys ignorance, the disturbing emotions and everything that is inimical to effective practice of the teachings. The hub, the rim and the spokes of the wheel represent respectively the training in ethical discipline, the training in concentration and the training in wisdom.

When teachings are requested it is customary to offer a mandala consisting of nine heaps. One heap is placed in the center of the base and the other eight heaps in the cardinal and intermediate directions. Normally the different heaps that are placed on the mandala base represent all the precious things in the universe but here the heaps represent a wheel with a hub and eight spokes. We imagine it to be the thousand-spoked golden wheel offered by Brahma.

37. *Madhyamakaśāstra*, *dBu ma'i bstan bcos*, P5224, Vol. 95. For an English translation of this text, see Jay L. Garfield, trans., *The Fundamental Wisdom of the Middle Way: Nagarjuna's Mūlamadhyamaka-Kārikā* (New York: Oxford University Press, 1995).

38. *rTen 'brel bstod pa*, P6016, Vol. 153. English translation in Robert Thurman, ed., *The Life and Teachings of Tsong Khapa* (Dharamsala: Library of Tibetan Works and Archives, 1982).

39. The transitory collection (*'jig tshogs*) refers to the body and mind, which undergo constant change and to which the validly existing self is attributed. This self is not perceived as it is but is distorted by the false view.

40. The four points are: ascertaining the object of refutation (*dgag bya nges pa'i gnad*), ascertaining the pervasion (*khyab pa nges pa'i gnad*) that there are only two ways in which what one is looking for could exist and that there are no further possibilities; ascertaining lack of truly existent oneness (*bden pa'i gcig bral du nges pa'i gnad*) and ascertaining lack of truly existent separateness or plurality (*bden pa'i du bral du nges pa'i gnad*).

41. Those who have made a formal commitment to take refuge in the Three Jewels for as long as they live observe certain precepts. The individual precepts concern what should and should not be done with

regard to each of the Three Jewels. The precepts in relation to the Buddha are that one should not consider any other refuge or source of protection higher than the Buddha and should respect all images of the Buddha and enlightened beings, whether or not they are well made or made of something precious.

The precepts in relation to the teachings are, as far as possible, not to harm other living beings and to respect all texts which contain instruction on what behavior and attitudes to adopt and what to discard, since they are intended for one's own and others' well being.

The precepts in relation to the spiritual community are not to allow one's physical, verbal or mental activity to be influenced by those who dislike and oppose the Buddha's teaching and to respect all members of the spiritual community, no matter which form of Buddhism they practice, regarding them as spiritual companions, offering them material help and fostering a relationship with them based on the teachings.

The general precepts are to take refuge again and again, remembering the special qualities and distinguishing features of the Three Jewels; to offer the first and best part of food and drink and to make other offerings, remembering the kindness of the Three Jewels; to encourage others, who show an interest, to take refuge; to entrust oneself to the Three Jewels in whatever activities one undertakes; not to give up the Three Jewels even in joke or at the cost on one's life; to take refuge three times each day and three times each night, remembering the benefits of doing so: (1) one becomes a Buddhist and (2) a suitable basis for all vows, (3) formerly accumulated karmic obstructions come to an end, (4) extensive stores of positive energy are easily accumulated, (5) harm from humans and non-humans cannot affect one, (6) one will not take bad rebirths, (7) one will accomplish all one's wishes, and (8) one will become enlightened quickly.

42. The seven-part practice consists of paying physical, verbal and mental homage to the enlightened ones, their teaching and to all those who possess noble qualities, presenting them with offerings, acknowledging wrong actions, rejoicing in one's own and others' virtue and good deeds, requesting the enlightened ones to teach in order to remove the darkness of ignorance, requesting them to remain in the world to guide and inspire living beings, and dedicating the positive energy created through this and other actions to become a cause for one's speedy attainment of highest enlightenment for the good of all.

43. One such position is that of Vairochana, which has seven features. (1) The legs are placed in the vajra position, which creates an auspicious precedent for attaining the vajra position of the energy channels,

winds and constituents during the stage of completion in the practice of tantra. Although this position is initially not easy to hold, it can be maintained for long periods when one is accustomed to it. Keeping the lower part of the body locked in this way prevents ailments caused by cold, but the upper part of the body should be as relaxed as possible to prevent disturbances of the energy winds. (2) The hands are in the position of meditative equipoise, four finger-widths below the navel, with the back of the left hand resting on the palm of the right. The thumbs touch, thereby creating a triangle. This position of the hands symbolizes activation of the psychic heat centered at the navel. (3) The elbows are kept away from the body to allow a flow of air under the arms, which prevents slackness and lethargy in meditation. (4) The spine is kept straight to bring the energy channels into the best position for free movement of the energy winds. (5) The chin is slightly tucked in to inhibit the upward-flowing energy winds, which cause agitation when uncontrolled. (6) The mouth is neither open nor tightly closed, but relaxed with the tip of the tongue touching the upper palate behind the front teeth. This prevents thirst and drooling during long periods of meditative absorption. (7) The eyes are neither wide open, which encourages distraction, nor tightly closed, which can lead to sleepiness. They are loosely focused in line with the tip of one's nose.

44. *Ocean of Reasoning, Explanation of "Treatise on the Middle Way"* (*dBu ma rtsa ba'i tshig le'ur byas pa shes rab ces bya ba'i rnam bshad rigs pa'i rgya mtsho,* P6153, Vol. 156) is also known as the *Great Commentary on Fundamental Wisdom* (*rTsa she tik chen*).

45. Jangkya Rolpay Dorjay (lCang skya rol pa'i rdo rje Ye shes bstan pa'i sgron me, 1717-1786) is best known now for his *Presentation of Tenets* (*Grub mtha'i rnam bzhag*). *Recognizing the Mother* (*A ma ngos 'dzin*) is also called the *Song of Experience of the View* (*lTa ba'i nyams mgur*). He bestowed teachings and initiations on the emperor of China, who honored him with a special title.

46. A valid cognition investigating conventionalities (*tha snad dpyod byed kyi tshad ma*) establishes the existence of phenomena other than the fundamental nature of things. A valid cognition which is a reasoning consciousness investigating the ultimate (*don dam dpyod byed kyi rigs shes*) establishes the fundamental way in which things exist.

47. *mnyam gzhag nam mkha' lta bu'i stong nyid.*

48. This is referred to as the subsequent illusion-like emptiness (*rjes thob sgyu ma lta bu'i stong nyid*).

49. Grasping at what is desired (*'dod pa nyer bar len pa*), grasping at views (*lta ba nyer bar len pa*) which include extreme views (*mthar lta*), wrong views (*log lta*) and holding false views as supreme (*lta ba mchog 'dzin*), grasping at ethics and discipline (*tshul khrims dang brtul zhugs nyer bar len pa*) and grasping at assertions of a self (*bdag tu smra ba nyer bar len pa*).

50. The twelve-part process of dependent arising (*rten 'brel yan lag bcu gnyis*) is normally presented in the following order: ignorance (*ma rigs pa*), formative action (*'du byed*), consciousness (*rnam par shes pa*), name and form (*ming gzugs*), the sources (*skyed mched*), contact (*reg pa*), feeling (*tshor ba*), craving (*sred pa*), grasping (*len pa*), existence (*srid pa*), birth (*skye ba*), ageing and death (*rga shi*).

51. The sixteen practices consist of thirteen prohibitions: restraint from the ten harmful actions as well as from drinking alcohol, adopting a bad source of livelihood and exercising violence. In addition to this one should give with respect to those in need, make gifts to those worthy of offerings and be loving.

52. For all schools of Buddhist philosophical tenets except Prasangika-Madhyamika the absence of a self which is a single, unitary, independent entity (*rtag gcig rang dbang can gyi bdag gis stong pa*) constitutes coarse selflessness of the person, and the absence of a self which is a self-sufficient substantially existent entity (*rang rkya thub pa'i rdzas su yod pa'i bdag gis stong pa*) is the subtle selflessness of the person. According to the Prasangika system the latter constitutes coarse selflessness of the person, while the subtle selflessness is the self's lack of inherent existence (*rang bzhin gyis grub pas stong pa*). No Buddhist school of thought accepts the existence of a self which is a single, unitary and independent entity. The idea of the self as a self-sufficient substantially existent entity presupposes a relationship between the self and the body and mind which is like that of a king and his court. The self is seen as the controller of the aggregates in the way that a king is distinct from and in charge of his court.

53. *Bhagavatīprajñāpāramitāhṛdayasūtra*, bCom ldan 'das ma shes rab kyi pha rol tu phyin pa'i snying po'i mdo, P160, Vol. 6. English translation in: Geshe Rabten, *Echoes of Voidness*, edited and translated by Stephen Batchelor (London: Wisdom, 1983).

54. The Tibetan word for nectar, *bdud rtsi*, literally means "demon remedy." *rTsi* is also used to denote elixir. Like an alchemical elixir the Buddha's precious teaching, particularly that on the nature of reality,

has the power to purify demonic obstructions and to transform the base metal of our present condition into the gold of liberation and enlightenment.

55. The five defining features are: it cannot be known by another (*gzhan las shes pa min*), it is pacification (*zhi ba*), it is unelaborated (*ma spros pa*), without conceptuality (*rnam rtog med pa*) and undifferentiated (*tha dad med pa*).

56. For exalted beings directly perceiving reality, no difference is experienced between the subjective awareness apprehending emptiness and the emptiness which is apprehended. The analogy which is used to describe the experience is of water poured into water. Ordinary people apprehend emptiness by way of a mental image and the apprehending awareness and what is apprehended are experienced as different. Here duality (*gnyis snang*) can be taken to refer to this.

57. *Illumination of the Thought, Extensive Explanation of (Chandrakirti's) "Supplement to the Middle Way"* (*dBu ma la 'jug pa'i rgya cher bshad pa dgongs pa rab gsal*, P6143, Vol. 154).

58. The verses of Nagarjuna's *Treatise on the Middle Way* are extremely terse and are open to varying interpretations. Here, the inner can be taken to refer to the conventionally existent self and the outer to the aggregates that are the basis of imputation for the self, as well as to external phenomena not associated with the mindstream of a living being.

59. This may also be interpreted to mean that reality, as it is experienced by exalted beings in meditative equipoise, cannot be expressed by language, since it is not within the mind's sphere of activity, inasmuch as conceptual thought cannot apprehend emptiness in the way that direct perception does. Another explanation is that emptiness, as perceived by the exalted beings in meditative equipoise, is beyond definition as this or that by language and mental activity.

60. Tsongkhapa explains this verse in terms of a gradual progression towards the understanding of reality. The last line, *yang dag min min yang dag min*, is extremely opaque. It can be taken to mean that things which are unreal in the sense of changing moment by moment are not inherently existent yet they are not non-existent because they undergo momentary change. Other interpretations explain that things are nominally real, ultimately unreal and to the mind of an exalted being in meditative equipoise neither real nor unreal.